CHILD ..... PLEASE..........

The story of truth, vision, and evidence of God's Purpose played out!

Dreams are Visions, even as a child.

Dr. Sharli Kay Marlow- Adair

DEDICATION PAGE

This book is dedicated to all the wonderful God-given villages that helped me survive. Many have gone to be with the Lord, but I salute you.

(Rest in Love)

Ms. Dorothy Marlow - Mother

Mr. Charlie Marlow - Father

Keith Steven Ingram – Brother

Mr. Edward Ingram – Grandfather

Mrs. Martha Ingram – Grandmother

Mrs. Fannie Mae Marlow- Grandmother

Mr. Terrance Taylor – God- Brother

Mr. Matthew Mitchell – God Brother

Ms. Lashundra Dowdy- Niece

Grateful for my Village of Love (Rest in Love)

Mother Bernice Brown

Mother Kathryn Rideout

Bishop Samuel and Mother Lee Ella Smith

Mr. Lepolia & Mrs. Ann Stewart

Mrs. Ann Norton

Mother Geneva Usher

Mother Recie Tinsley

TABLE OF CONTENTS

DEDICATION PAGE 2

OPENING PRAYER: 4

INTRODUCTION 5

CHAPTER 1: DON'T WORRY! IT MADE ME WHO I AM TODAY! 8

CHAPTER 2: WAIT VS. WEIGHT — LOVING MYSELF THROUGH THE JOURNEY - MORE THAN MY WEIGHT. 28

CHAPTER 3: DEGREES OF CONFIDENCE 42

CHAPTER 4: GOD SEE YOU 54

CHAPTER 5: THE O ZONE- OCCUPYING THE ZONE OF OPPORTUNITY 59

CHAPTER 6: LOVE IS NOT LOVE UNTIL YOU LOVE! 76

CHAPTER 7: EAGLE WINGS... EAGLE VISION 87

CHAPTER 8: GRUDGES YOU MUST RELEASE - LEARNING HOW TO HEAL, RELEASE, AND KEEP MOVING 100

CHAPTER 9: CHILD, PLEASE — YOU CAN MAKE IT 110

ANCHOR SCRIPTURES FOR DR SHARLI K. ADAIR 129

CLOSING PRAYER 130

ACKNOWLEDGEMENT 131

OPENING PRAYER:

Heavenly Father,

Before I speak or write a word, I invite You into this moment. Let this testimony not be about me, but about You -Your faithfulness, Your voice, and Your purpose. Thank You for speaking to me, even when I was too young to fully understand. Thank You for holding me through pain, showing me hope through dreams, and lifting me above what tried to break me. May these words reflect Your glory and speak life to someone who needs to be reminded that You still speak, that You still see, and that You still save. Use my story to reveal your heart.

In Jesus' name, Amen.

INTRODUCTION

Even as a child, God can speak to you clearly, no matter how difficult your life may be. Hardships, pain, or broken surroundings do not limit His voice - He often uses those very struggles to draw you closer to Him. In moments when everything feels uncertain or overwhelming, God can give you peace that doesn't make sense to the world. He reminds you that you're not forgotten, and that He sees the whole picture of your life even when you can't. God's voice can be gentle, like a whisper to your heart, or powerful through Scripture, people, or even nature, but one way He often speaks to children is through dreams. That is my truth, he spoke to me clearly as a child in clear, recurring, identical dreams.

God has always used dreams to reveal His plans, even to the young- just like He did with Joseph in the Bible. When you're still growing and discovering who you are, God might show you glimpses of your purpose through dreams, visions, or deep feelings that won't go away. These are not just your imagination; they can be God planting seeds for the future He's preparing for you. Even when life feels unfair or confusing, God is already shaping your journey and calling you into something greater. Children are not too young to hear from

God—in fact, their faith and openness often make them the perfect vessels for His voice.

Children are **not** too young to hear from God. In fact, Scripture consistently shows us that God not only values children but also often chooses to speak through them and to them. Jesus Himself affirmed this in Matthew 19:14 when He said, *"Let the little children come to me, and do not hinder them, for the kingdom of heaven belongs to such as these."* Children carry an innocence and purity of heart that makes them especially sensitive to the voice of God. Their faith is often unfiltered, unshaped by doubt, and open to the supernatural in ways that adults can easily miss. God sees their hearts, and He is more than capable of planting seeds of purpose, vision, and understanding in them—even at a young age.

Throughout the Bible, God uses children and young people in powerful ways. Samuel, for example, heard God's voice as a child while serving in the temple under Eli (1 Samuel 3). He didn't fully understand at first, but when guided and affirmed, Samuel responded to God's call, saying, *"Speak, Lord, for your servant is listening."* That one encounter marked the beginning of his prophetic ministry. This reminds us that God not only speaks to children, but He does so with purpose—to raise them, shape them, and use them. We must never overlook or dismiss what a child says when it is rooted in spiritual insight or genuine curiosity about God. Instead, we should nurture it, encourage it, and affirm their ability to connect with their Creator.

Children are *precious* to God, and He speaks life into them in ways that are gentle yet profound. He can speak through a dream, a whisper in prayer, a scripture they hear in Sunday school, or even through their own thoughts and questions. Our role as parents, leaders, and mentors is to create space for them to hear God and to help them recognize His voice. Proverbs 22:6 empowers us with the reminder: *"Train up a child in the way he should go, and when he is old, he will not depart from it."* That training includes teaching children to listen for God, to trust His voice, and to know that they are never too small, too young, or too inexperienced to have a real relationship with Him. When children understand that they can hear from God, it plants boldness in their identity and faith in their future.

Allow this book to bless and encourage you to move forward.

CHAPTER 1: DON'T WORRY! IT MADE ME WHO I AM TODAY!

Soaring Above: Father's Struggle, A Child's Strength, God's Unfailing Love, and God's Redeeming Voice

From my earliest years, even in the middle of my most painful and frightening moments, I sensed that my life was not an accident. I say this not out of arrogance, but out of deep reverence and gratitude: I am sure that God purposed my life. That confidence came despite an imperfect upbringing and a turbulent environment. My childhood was marked by fear, trauma, and confusion. But even in the mess, God was there, speaking to me through dreams, through people, and through the quiet inner voice that whispered, *You are loved. You will rise.*

My father was a functioning alcoholic. He worked hard. He provided for our family. He demanded education, respect, and obedience. From the outside, many would have seen him as a strong, responsible man. And in some ways, he was. But behind closed doors, the atmosphere was scary. His words - often harsh, unpredictable, and laced with hard foul language. On the weekends, along with those words, he would be drenched in alcohol from Friday night through Sunday. This left lasting wounds on my spirit. It was a home where fear lived alongside discipline, where love was not spoken but shown in food, a clean home, clean clothes, and other ways a child could understand. Though alcohol was his demon, he somehow managed to function Monday through Friday, showing up for work, fulfilling duties, and maintaining an image that things were "under control." This strange duality, *dysfunction wrapped in discipline*, can be confusing for those who grow up in it. Because when someone's brokenness is masked by routine, it blurs the line between normal and toxic.

This is the reality of what's often called *high-function dysfunction*. A person can appear stable to the outside world while privately battling inner turmoil, addiction, or unresolved trauma. For the children and family members in that environment, it creates a conflicting experience: "We had rules, but we also had fear. We had structure, but not safety. We had presence, but not peace." That's the complexity of growing up in a home where someone can hold down a job and still be bound by addiction. The functioning becomes a cover—a way of proving, both to others and to themselves, that they're "fine." But functioning doesn't equal healing. And discipline without love or safety creates confusion, not character.

A Woman of Faith and Strength- Praying Mother

Although my father struggled with alcoholism—a battle that often brought pain and moments of domestic violence into our home—my mother remained steadfast. Through every trial, she stood as a pillar of faith, maintaining our household, caring for six children, working a full-time job, and faithfully serving in her church every Sunday and throughout the week.

My mother was a true *prayer warrior*, a woman who knew how to touch heaven on behalf of her family. Her prayers were the covering that kept us safe, her faith the anchor that held us steady.

The Bible says in **Proverbs 31:25-28 (KJV)**:

"Strength and honour are her clothing, and she shall rejoice in time to come. She openeth her mouth with wisdom; and in her tongue is the law of kindness... Her children arise up, and call her blessed; her husband also, and he praiseth her." KJV

My mother lived this scripture daily. Despite hardship, she walked in strength and dignity. She faced adversity with grace and refused to let bitterness take root.

Like the persistent widow in **Luke 18:1–8**, she never ceased praying, trusting that God would bring justice, healing, and provision in due time. Her faith in God's promises reminded us that *"The effectual fervent prayer of a righteous [woman] availeth much"* (**James 5:16**).

Even in chaos, she carried the *peace of God, which surpasses all understanding* (**Philippians 4:7**). Her love was patient and steadfast, reflecting the heart of Christ in our home.

Truly, my mother was a woman of God—powerful in spirit, unwavering in faith, and full of love and integrity. Her life was a living testimony that, no matter the storm, God's grace is sufficient, and His strength is made perfect in weakness (**2 Corinthians 12:9**).

I often wondered, even as a small child, *how my mother did it.* How did she carry so much, yet still stand so strong, love so deeply, and give so freely? In my young heart, I made her a promise — that when I grew up, I would build houses for her, so she would never again have to live in the difficult situations we once knew.

My mother taught us what it truly meant to love, no matter the circumstances. She would always say, "Make your corner bright, no matter how dark it may seem." That became more than just words — it was how she lived.

There were days when the lights would be turned off because the bills couldn't be paid. Yet my mother had a way of turning those moments into joy. She would spread blankets on the floor, make pallets for us to sleep on, and tell stories or sing songs. We laughed together, not even realizing at times that we were sitting in the dark. What could have been a moment of shame became a memory of love — because she filled the darkness with light.

Her faith never wavered. Every Sunday — no matter what the week had been like — she had us dressed and ready for church. She taught us that God was our provider, our protector, and our peace. Her steadfast spirit began to change the very atmosphere of our home. Over time, I began to see my father change, too. Her unmovable faith and strong, gentle spirit touched his heart.

My mother's labor was not in vain. Her prayers, her endurance, and her unwavering faith planted seeds that blossomed in all of us. She embodied the truth of **Philippians 4:11-13**, living content and grateful in every circumstance: "I have learned, in whatsoever state I am, therewith to be content... I can do all things through Christ, which strengtheneth me." KJV

Even in hardship, she taught us joy. Even in lack, she showed us abundance. And even in darkness, she showed us the light of Christ.

Truly, my mother was a reflection of **Matthew 5:16**: "Let your light so shine before men, that they may see your good works, and glorify your Father which is in heaven." Her life was that light — steady, glowing, and unwavering — guiding us through every shadow.

Seeing Myself Through Heaven's Eyes: Trusting God's Plan for My Future

There are moments in life when everything seems to freeze in time, and you catch a glimpse of a deeper reality, something beyond the physical world, something spiritual and true. I remember such a moment vividly. It was as though I could look down and see myself—not as I am now, but as I was: a child in distress, surrounded, overwhelmed, trapped in a fog of confusion and fear. Yet even in that moment of helplessness, something miraculous was happening. I was also flying—rising above chaos, unburdened, looking down with clarity and peace. It was as if God had lifted me to show me a truth that I couldn't see from the ground: that even in my confusion, I was not abandoned. I was seen, known, and held. When God speaks to you as a child, He marks you with purpose. He lets you know—even if only through whispers, visions, or a deep sense of His presence—that your future is secure in Him. That moment becomes a spiritual anchor, a divine reminder that your life is not random or forgotten. It means He has placed His hand upon you, and no matter what path your life takes, His fingerprints will remain.

As children, we are especially open to the voice of God. Our hearts have not yet been hardened by cynicism, disappointment, or pride. We are naturally inclined to trust, to believe in the unseen, to hope beyond reason. That is why when God reaches out to us in childhood, it is such a powerful and lasting encounter. He knows the journey ahead, and He begins planting seeds early. He speaks into our young hearts' words of identity, love, and destiny. And while we may not fully understand those words at the time, they remain like hidden treasures, waiting to be unearthed in due season. In Scripture, we are reminded repeatedly that God cares deeply for children. Jesus said, *"Let the little children come to me, and do not hinder them, for the kingdom of heaven belongs to such as these"* (Matthew 19:14). God doesn't see children as insignificant or immature—He sees them as examples of the kind of faith we are all called to embody. When God speaks to a child, He isn't being simplistic—He's being strategic. He's shaping a future.

The promise of Jeremiah 29:11 rings true here: *"For I know the plans I have for you," declares the Lord, "plans to prosper you and not to harm you, plans to give you hope and a future."* This is not just a general promise for a nation—it's a personal assurance for every child who dares to trust Him. When God declares that He has a plan for your life, He's not merely speaking of a vague destiny; He's speaking of a carefully crafted path that leads you through valleys and victories, molding you along the way into the person He designed you to be. And yet, trusting in that plan isn't always easy, especially when you're young and life is confusing. When you're surrounded by struggle, when adults fail you, when the world seems harsh and cold, it can be difficult to reconcile the pain you see with the promise you've heard. But here's the truth: God does not abandon the ones He calls. His presence is not dependent on your ability to understand, but on His unwavering commitment to be with you.

Even in moments when you feel forgotten or overlooked, God is still working behind the scenes. His plan is still unfolding, and His hand is still guiding you. That feeling of being "above it all"—that moment of spiritual clarity—is often God's way of reminding you that your life is bigger than the moment you're in. It's His way of lifting your eyes from your current pain to His eternal promise. This is why childlike trust is so vital. It doesn't mean you never question or feel afraid. It means that deep down, you choose to believe that God is who He says He is, a loving Father, a faithful Guide, a constant Presence. It means that when you look into your future, you do not see only uncertainty, but divine potential. Trusting God as a child sets the foundation for trusting Him as an adult. It creates a history between you and Him, a sacred bond of faith that matures over time. The promises spoken to your young heart become the pillars that hold you up when life gets hard. And one day, you may look back and realize that every detour, every delay, every season of pain had purpose. That nothing was wasted. That the voice you heard as a child—the one that said, "You are mine. I have a plan for you" was true all along.

So to the child within you, to the one who may still be hurting or wondering or waiting, hear this: God sees you. He knows the confusion and the questions. But more importantly, He holds your future. And it is good. It is full of hope. You don't have to figure everything out—you only have to trust. Because when God speaks to you as a child, He is not just speaking to your present; He is speaking to your destiny. Although fear was a reality, I never stopped experiencing the voice of God as a child. In the scariest and darkest seasons of my life, God gave me dreams. Starting at 7 years old, I would dream of my body rising, soaring like an aircraft - powerful, unstoppable, majestic.

In those dreams, I could look down and see myself as I was: a child in distress, surrounded, trapped in confusion. But I was also flying, free above all. God was giving me a glimpse of His plan for me, even when I couldn't make sense of it. He was showing me that though my circumstances were broken, I was not broken beyond repair. I would rise, like an eagle — in fact, in some dreams, I flew even *higher* than the eagle.

What fascinated me most in those dreams was how clearly I could see. I could look down and see the whole picture — the trauma, the dysfunction, and the child I was becoming. This wasn't just physical sight. It was a *vision*. God was showing me something profound: I would rise, yes, but I would also *see*. I would understand. I would gain wisdom beyond my years, shaped not just by pain, but by the One who called me to fly.

It took me time to understand this: my father loved me, but only to the capacity that he was able to love. His alcoholism and his own inner wounds limited how he showed that love. His addiction, his pain, and possibly even his own unhealed wounds limited how he expressed that love. That realization didn't erase the trauma, but it helped me release the bitterness. His pain did not excuse his actions, but it helped me stop blaming myself. His love was flawed, but I wasn't unlovable. And just because his expression of love was broken didn't mean God's love would be, but it helped me understand that his brokenness did not mean I was unworthy of true love. His inability to show love in healthy ways did not define my value. And most importantly, it did not have to destroy me.

God showed me love through others. Teachers who believed in me. Family members who showed kindness. Friends and Church members who became safe spaces. And always, through dreams — where God, like a Father who sees all, reminded me, *"You are not forgotten. You are not alone. And you will not stay here forever."* Even now, I realize: my father taught strength, but God taught me how to use it with wisdom and grace. My father demanded obedience, but God invited me into a *relationship*. My father instilled fear, but God gave me faith. I am not who I am today despite what I went through — I am who I am *because* God redeemed what I went through. Today, I look back not to relive the pain, but to remember the victory. I can acknowledge the damage while still celebrating the deliverance. I can admit my father's failures without denying his humanity. And I can stand as living proof that what the enemy tried to use to destroy me, God is now using to build something beautiful — a life of purpose, perspective, and unshakable faith.

The flight became more than a symbol in my dreams. It became a spiritual truth. Not only would I rise, but I would also see- an unimaginable vision. Eyes trained to spot what others miss, eyes that discern the path ahead. God was giving me more than hope; He was giving me vision. The ability to see life with spiritual understanding. The capacity to look at pain and still see purpose. To face brokenness and still believe in beauty. To remember trauma and still walk in healing.

Somewhere along the way, I stopped flying only in my dreams — and started rising in real life. I began to believe that my life mattered. That my voice was important. That I didn't have to repeat the patterns I was born into. I learned that the past is not a prison when God holds the key. And though I still carry the memories, I no longer carry the shame. My father's words once pierced me -but now, God's words define me. His love is louder. His dreams are bigger. His vision is clearer. And His promises are sure.

So if you're reading this and you've lived under the weight of someone else's broken love — know this: **God's love is not limited by theirs.** Your story doesn't end in dysfunction. You can rise. You can heal. You can forgive. And you can fly — not just in your dreams, but in your destiny.

Forgiveness wasn't forgetting or pretending it didn't hurt. It was letting go of the power that pain had over my identity. It was choosing healing, over and over again. And in that process, God continued to speak - through dreams where I was lifted above it all, where I could see the trauma below me but know in my spirit that I was rising higher. I wasn't bound to repeat the cycle. I wasn't destined to stay broken.

Don't Die in the Process

Growth is painful. It stretches you, challenges you, and often pushes you past your comfort zone. There will be moments when it feels like you're being crushed under the weight of your own process—but that's not the end. In fact, pressure is often the very thing that produces purpose. Just like a seed has to be buried in darkness before it breaks through the soil, your process may feel like a burial, but it's really a planting. Don't give up. Don't shut down. Don't mistake pain for punishment. You're being shaped for something bigger than where you are right now. The growth hurts, but it's also what's keeping you alive and preparing you for what's ahead.

Don't complain—use it. Complaining only drains energy and magnifies the problem. But when you choose to *use* the trial, to *learn* from it, and to *grow* through it, you shift from being a victim to being victorious. Philippians 2:14 tells us, *"Do* *everything without grumbling or arguing."* That's not because God wants you to stay silent, but because complaining blocks perspective. It keeps you focused on what's wrong instead of seeing what God might be doing *through* it. Instead of asking, "Why me?" try asking, "What is this teaching me?" Everything you go through has the potential to build something in you—resilience, compassion, wisdom, humility.

Everything you go through has the potential to *build something in you*. Every storm, every heartbreak, every trial — none of it is wasted. In the process of pain, God is producing something powerful: **resilience, compassion, wisdom, and humility.**

But hear this — *don't die in the process.*

Don't let your spirit die while you're still living. Don't let your love, your joy, or your respect for yourself fade away. Even when life breaks you down, use those broken pieces to build again. Use what hurt you to *help you*. Use what tried to destroy you to *develop you*.

When Joseph was betrayed by his brothers and thrown into a pit, it could have killed his spirit — but he didn't die in the process. What the enemy meant for evil, God turned for good (**Genesis 50:20**). The pit was preparation for the palace.

There are moments when the weight of life feels unbearable — when you think you can't make it another day. But that's when you remind yourself: *God didn't bring me this far to leave me here.*

Psalm 118:17 says,

"I shall not die, but live, and declare the works of the Lord."

That verse is your declaration: you will *live* when you were supposed to die. The pain didn't kill you; it pushed you closer to your purpose.

Every time you survived what was meant to destroy you, it was proof that there's *still destiny inside of you.* God's hand is still on your life.

Isaiah 43:2 reminds us: "When thou passest through the waters, I will be with thee; and through the rivers, they shall not overflow thee: when thou walkest through the fire, thou shalt not be burned."

You may walk *through* fire, but you won't be consumed. You may walk *through* the valley, but you will not die there. God is still writing your story, and every hard chapter is shaping you for the victory that's coming.

Hold on. Don't die in the process. Keep praying. Keep loving. Keep believing. Use the pain to push you into purpose. Use the process to produce power.

And when you come out — and you *will* come out — you'll be able to say with confidence: "It was good for me that I have been afflicted; that I might learn thy statutes." — **Psalm 119:71**

You lived when you were supposed to die — not just to survive, but to *testify* that God is still faithful.

Don't waste your pain. Let it develop you.

Use your growth to treat others the way God treats them.

One of the greatest results of a trial is the softening of your heart toward others. When you've walked through hardship and seen how God met you with grace, it changes how you handle people. You begin to see others not through judgment, but through mercy. You learn to lead with kindness, patience, and love—not because they earned it, but because *you've been there too.* God doesn't just grow us for our own sake; He grows us so we can reflect Him to others. 2 Corinthians 1:4 says God *"comforts us in all our troubles, so that we can comfort those in any trouble with the comfort we ourselves receive from God."* Your pain has purpose—not just for you, but for everyone you'll one day encourage.

Life has a way of teaching us lessons we never asked to learn. Many of us have walked through storms that shaped us, seasons that broke us, and moments that changed us forever. But the greatest testimony is not that we survived — it's that we came out better, softer, wiser, and more loving than before.

What I went through made me decide that I would use my growth to treat people the way *God* treats them — with love, compassion, and forgiveness. I learned that pain has two choices: it can make you bitter, or it can make you better.

As a child, love was not always my testimony. There were moments when I didn't feel seen, protected, or valued. But even then, *God saw me.* He kept my heart from hardening completely. He gave me hope when I didn't even know His name fully. That same hope became the seed of my healing. When God heals you, He doesn't just patch up your wounds — He transforms your heart. He teaches you how to love right, even when love was not modeled for you. He teaches you how to extend grace, even when grace was not extended to you. And He reminds you that every storm you survived was not meant to make you cruel, but compassionate.

The Bible says in **Ephesians 4:32 (KJV)**:

"And be ye kind one to another, tenderhearted, forgiving one another, even as God for Christ's sake hath forgiven you." That verse became a foundation for me. It reminded me that kindness is not weakness — it's strength under control. Forgiveness is not forgetting what happened — it's refusing to let what happened define how I treat others.

I manage right because of the storm I came through. I love right because I know what it feels like to live without love. My storms didn't destroy me; they disciplined me. They taught me to see people through the lens of grace instead of judgment.

When you've been through enough pain, you begin to recognize pain in others — and instead of reacting, you respond with empathy. You start to understand that people's actions often come from their own unhealed places. That understanding is what allows you to treat them like God does: with mercy.

I live my deliverance out loud. I love intentionally. I speak gently. I forgive quickly. Because what I've been through taught me that life is fragile, people are precious, and God's love is the only standard worth following.

I'm not who I was — and that's the proof that God can use your pain to teach you how to treat people right.

Know that your trial shaped you and positioned you for greatness.

Nothing you've been through is wasted. The sleepless nights, the silent battles, the closed doors—they all contributed to your strength and clarity today. Romans 8:28 reminds us that *"in all things God works for the good of those who love him."* Your trial didn't break you—it built you. It pulled out the version of you that you didn't know existed. And now that you've survived the storm, you're positioned for more: more purpose, more influence, more clarity, and more capacity to walk in greatness. Don't resent the process—*honor* it.

Winning doesn't always look like applause, trophies, or public success. Sometimes, winning looks like *getting out of bed when you didn't feel like it*. Sometimes it looks like *choosing to forgive when it would've been easier to stay bitter.* You win every time you choose peace over chaos, growth over comfort, and faith over fear. Life may not have handed you ideal circumstances, but your ability to keep going, to keep believing, and to keep becoming—*that's victory*. The enemy didn't win. Your past didn't win. The depression didn't win. *You did.* Just by standing, surviving, and striving to be better, you've proven that you are not defined by what happened to you. You're defined by what you *did with it*.

Winners fall, but they don't stay down. Proverbs 24:16 says, *"For though the righteous fall seven times, they rise again."* That's what makes you a winner—not perfection, but persistence. You've had setbacks, delays, maybe even detours, but you never quit. That's what champions do—they may bend, but they don't break. And even when you felt broken, God was building you back up, stronger than before. Winning isn't about having the easiest road; it's about finishing the race marked out for *you*. Every time you got up when it would've been easier to give up, you declared, *"I win,* "Because the very thing that tried to destroy you was what God used to *develop* you. Keep growing. Keep loving. Keep rising. Live by any God given means necessary.

CHAPTER 2: WAIT VS. WEIGHT – LOVING MYSELF THROUGH THE JOURNEY - MORE THAN MY WEIGHT

I carried more than just physical weight growing up — I carried the **weight of waiting**. Waiting to be accepted. Waiting to feel loved, waiting to feel beautiful in a world that told me I wasn't. For most of my childhood and adolescence, I was morbidly obese. That's the clinical term, but what it really meant was that I was constantly looked at… and overlooked at the same time. People saw the body, but they didn't see the person inside it.

From a very early age, I was made to feel like I was too much — too heavy, too big, too loud, too visible, yet somehow invisible at the same time. I remember moments where I felt like I was in the room, but not really *in* it. I wasn't chosen for games at recess. I wasn't invited to birthday parties. I was often the target of whispers or loud laughter. I can still hear the mockery in the hallways — names I never asked for, comments no one should ever hear. But through it all, I made a vow to myself: *I will not have low self-esteem. I will love all of me, even when they don't.*

I still remember the stares, the jokes whispered just loud enough for me to hear, the way people would overlook me like I didn't matter. In group settings, I was the last one chosen. In classrooms, I was often overlooked. Even in friendships, I felt like the sidekick — never the one anyone celebrated. I learned how to shrink my presence emotionally while growing physically. I made jokes about myself before others could. I put on smiles that hid how much I was hurting inside.

But in all that pain, I made a quiet vow: *"I may be big, but I will not have small self-esteem. I will love all of me — even if no one else does"*.

I didn't fully know how to live that vow at the time, but deep down, something in me refused to be defined by other people's opinions. I was more than my body. I had a soul, a mind, a purpose. And even if no one else saw it — **God did**. He saw me.

"The Lord does not look at the things people look at. People look at the outward appearance, but the Lord looks at the heart." – 1 Samuel 16:7

Still, it was hard. The emotional weight of rejection added layers to the physical weight I already carried. It's a cycle many don't understand: the more you're mocked, the more you retreat. The more invisible you feel, the more comfort you seek. And for me, like so many others, food became that comfort. Not because I was greedy or lazy, but because it was consistent. It didn't judge me. It didn't exclude me. It didn't laugh at me. It was there — and I was hurting.

The **weight** was real, but the **wait** — that ache to be seen, heard, understood — was even heavier.

There were nights I cried silently, pillows soaking with unspoken pain. I didn't cry because I was big — I cried because I felt small. I turned inward. I began to build a protective shell around myself — emotionally and physically. I smiled in public, joked about myself before others could, and acted like it didn't bother me. But inside, I was in a battle no one could see.

But somewhere in the middle of that battle, something in me began to shift. Maybe it was maturity. Maybe it was the quiet prayers I whispered at night. Maybe it was God planting strength in me that would bloom over time. I don't know exactly when it started, but I remember the feeling: *I am tired of shrinking my dreams to fit the box others put me in. I am tired of waiting for permission to love myself. I will fight — not just to lose weight, but to gain freedom.*

That's when I began to understand the difference between **losing weight** and **living well.**

This wasn't about getting skinny to impress people who didn't care about my heart. It wasn't about changing my body to fit into a culture that constantly shifts its definition of beauty. It was about honoring the body God gave me — because I was worth the care. **Loving myself meant making choices that reflected that love.**

I had to relearn everything: not just how to eat or move, but how to think. How to speak to myself. How to stop punishing my body with shame and start partnering with it through healing. I had to make peace with food, peace with the mirror, and peace with the girl I had spent so many years criticizing. And no, it wasn't fast. It wasn't glamorous. I stumbled many times. But every small win was a whisper from God: *Keep going, daughter. You're worth the wait.*

In It for the WIN - How I Fought Back

I didn't transform overnight. I didn't wake up one morning with a flat stomach and a healed heart. It was slow. Messy. Beautiful. Painful. Sacred. I started walking — both literally and figuratively. Walking away from people who hurt me. Walking toward goals scared me. Walking through mental strongholds and tearing them down with Scripture. Walking with my head a little higher, even when I didn't feel worthy.

I changed how I spoke to myself. I stopped calling myself names in private that I would never tolerate from others. I started celebrating small victories: choosing water over soda, getting outside, going to therapy, saying "no" when I used to say "yes" just to please people.

I started showing up — for *me*. Not for applause. Not for approval. Just for the little girl inside me who waited so long to feel worthy.

I carried more than just physical weight growing up — I carried the **weight of waiting**. Waiting to be accepted. Waiting to feel loved, waiting to feel beautiful in a world that told me I wasn't. For most of my childhood and adolescence, I was morbidly obese. That's the clinical term, but what it really meant was that I was constantly looked at… and overlooked at the same time. People saw the body, but they didn't see the person inside it.

From a very early age, I was made to feel like I was too much — too heavy, too big, too loud, too visible, yet somehow invisible at the same time. I remember moments where I felt like I was in the room, but not really *in* it. I wasn't chosen for games at recess. I wasn't invited to birthday parties. I was often the target of whispers or loud laughter. I can still hear the mockery in the hallways — names I never asked for, comments no one should ever hear. But through it all, I made a vow to myself: *I will not have low self-esteem. I will love all of me, even when they don't.*

I still remember the stares, the jokes whispered just loud enough for me to hear, the way people would overlook me like I didn't matter. In group settings, I was the last one chosen. In classrooms, I was often overlooked. Even in friendships, I felt like the sidekick — never the one anyone celebrated. I learned how to shrink my presence emotionally while growing physically. I made jokes about myself before others could. I put on smiles that hid how much I was hurting inside.

But in all that pain, I made a quiet vow: "*I may be big, but I will not have small self-esteem. I will love all of me — even if no one else does*".

I didn't fully know how to live that vow at the time, but deep down, something in me refused to be defined by other people's opinions. I was more than my body. I had a soul, a mind, a purpose. And even if no one else saw it — **God did**. He saw me.

"The Lord does not look at the things people look at. People look at the outward appearance, but the Lord looks at the heart." – 1 Samuel 16:7

Still, it was hard. The emotional weight of rejection added layers to the physical weight I already carried. It's a cycle many don't understand: the more you're mocked, the more you retreat. The more invisible you feel, the more comfort you seek. And for me, like so many others, food became that comfort. Not because I was greedy or lazy, but because it was consistent. It didn't judge me. It didn't exclude me. It didn't laugh at me. It was there — and I was hurting.

The **weight** was real, but the **wait** — that ache to be seen, heard, understood — was even heavier.

There were nights I cried silently, pillows soaking with unspoken pain. I didn't cry because I was big — I cried because I felt small. I turned inward. I began to build a protective shell around myself — emotionally and physically. I smiled in public, joked about myself before others could, and acted like it didn't bother me. But inside, I was in a battle no one could see.

But somewhere in the middle of that battle, something in me began to shift. Maybe it was maturity. Maybe it was the quiet prayers I whispered at night. Maybe it was God planting strength in me that would bloom over time. I don't know exactly when it started, but I remember the feeling: *I am tired of shrinking my dreams to fit the box others put me in. I am tired of waiting for permission to love myself. I will fight — not just to lose weight, but to gain freedom.*

That's when I began to understand the difference between **losing weight** and **living well**.

This wasn't about getting skinny to impress people who didn't care about my heart. It wasn't about changing my body to fit into a culture that constantly shifts its definition of beauty. It was about honoring the body God gave me — because I was worth the care. **Loving myself meant making choices that reflected that love.**

I had to relearn everything: not just how to eat or move, but how to think. How to speak to myself. How to stop punishing my body with shame and start partnering with it through healing. I had to make peace with food, peace with the mirror, and peace with the girl I had spent so many years criticizing. And no, it wasn't fast. It wasn't glamorous. I stumbled many times. But every small win was a whisper from God: *Keep going, daughter. You're worth the wait.*

The Hurt Behind the Hunger

The truth is, I didn't become obese just because I liked food. I became obese because food was the only thing that didn't hurt me. It didn't laugh at me. It didn't bully me. It didn't ignore me. It was always there when people weren't. And so, I turned to it again and again. When I felt unlovable, food comforted me. When I felt powerless, food gave me control. When I felt empty, food filled the silence.

But hunger was never really for food — it was for **belonging**, **security**, **affection**, **identity**. I was feeding a wound that couldn't be healed with sugar or salt. And what made it harder was that no one saw the emotional weight I carried — only the physical weight I wore on my body.

The emotional toll became heavier than the number on any scale. The **wait to be accepted** became heavier than the actual **weight** on my body. That kind of waiting wears down your confidence. It builds walls around your heart. It makes you question your worth — and it keeps you stuck in survival mode.

The Turning Point: From Shame to Strength

There came a moment, slowly but strong, when I realized something had to change. Not just the number on the scale, but the **way I saw myself**. I was tired of waiting to be loved. Tired of waiting for people's approval. Tired of shrinking emotionally while expanding physically. I wanted more. Not just to look different, but to *live differently*.

That's when I started understanding the difference between:

- Weight loss and wholeness
- Looking good and living well
- Fitting in and walking in freedom

You see, weight loss is only one part of the story — but **healing** is the goal. Because you can lose 100 pounds and still carry shame, you can change your size and still hate your reflection. You can change your body and still not love your life. What I needed — what we *all* need — was to go deeper. To confront the pain, the beliefs, the lies, and the habits that kept me bound.

And that's when I realized: **loving myself isn't about ego — it's about survival. It's about stewardship. It's about choosing to live instead of just existing.**

Loving Yourself Enough to Live

Loving yourself doesn't mean ignoring your flaws. It means embracing your worth *while* working on your wellness. It means saying:

- "I am worth taking care of."
- "I am worth showing up for."
- "I don't have to wait to love myself — I can love myself into change."

And it's not just physical. Loving yourself means nourishing your mind with truth, your spirit with God's Word, your emotions with grace, and your body with movement, rest, and real food.

It's not about being "skinny." It's about being *alive*.

"I have come that they may have life, and have it to the full." – John 10:10

God doesn't want us just surviving. He wants us *to thrive*. Not for vanity's sake — but because we were made in His image. And if He thought we were worth dying for, how dare we treat ourselves like we're worthless?

When They Didn't Expect It… I Did It Anyway

Many people didn't expect me to change. Some were surprised I kept the weight off. Others were shocked to see me speak in front of crowds, lead, coach, or inspire. Some people only knew the "old" version of me — the one who hid, apologized for existing, or laughed to avoid crying.

But I've achieved things they didn't expect — not because I had to prove anything to them, but because **I stopped waiting** for permission to be great.

I started walking in the calling God gave me. And when you do that — when you live loved — the weight you lose is more than just pounds. You lose guilt. You lose shame. You lose fear. You lose the lie that says, *"You'll never be enough."*

Because in Christ, I am more than enough. And so are you. If you're reading this and you've ever felt "too much" or "not enough" — hear me: You are *already* enough. But you are also worthy of becoming more. **Not because you hate who you are, but because you love yourself enough to grow.**

Choosing to love yourself means choosing to do better — not just for how you look, but for how you *live*.

- So choose to rest.
- Choose to eat better.
- Choose to move your body.
- Choose therapy.
- Choose boundaries.
- Choose prayer.
- Choose joy.
- Choose truth.
- **Choose you.**

Because God already has.

I fought back- not just physically, but emotionally and mentally. I started setting boundaries. I stopped letting people speak to me in any kind of way. I stopped trying to be invisible in rooms where I had every right to belong. I started walking, then running, then doing things I never thought my body could do. People were shocked. Some had already written me off — assumed I'd always be "the big one," the quiet one, the sidekick in life's story. But I am writing my own story now. And I was walking it out — pound by pound, step by step, truth by truth.

One of my proudest moments wasn't the number on a scale or a before-and-after photo. It was standing in front of a group of people and speaking — confidently, boldly. No jokes to soften it. No shame in my voice. Just truth. I had achieved something others didn't expect. *I found peace with myself.* I didn't have to wait to be accepted. I accepted myself — and that acceptance became the foundation for every other healthy change that followed.

What I learned is this: **the world teaches us to chase weight loss for approval, but God teaches us to pursue wholeness for His glory.** This is not just about looking good. It's about living well. It's about waking up and feeling free — not trapped in shame or fear. It's about honoring your body as a temple, not a trophy. It's about loving yourself enough to stop settling for survival and start choosing life.

"I praise You because I am fearfully and wonderfully made; Your works are wonderful, I know that full well." – Psalm 139:14

And yes, the scale has moved. Yes, my clothes fit differently. Yes, people treat me differently now — but those are side effects, not the goal. The real victory is that I'm not waiting anymore. I'm living. I'm choosing me — not in a selfish way, but in a holy way. I'm choosing to show up for myself because God has called me, chosen me, and filled me with purpose.

So, if you're where I once was — in the middle of the weight and the wait — hear me: **You are not broken. You are not lazy. You are not unlovable. You are worthy of care, worthy of love, and worthy of healing.** Don't let the world define you by numbers, comments, or expectations. Let God define you by truth.

And that truth says: *You are enough. You are fearfully and wonderfully made. And you are not alone. 1 Samuel 16:7 – "Man looks at the outward appearance, but the Lord looks at the heart."*

CHAPTER 3: DEGREES OF CONFIDENCE

Who, Me? Yes, you — Called to Be Better.

I didn't think I was smart., I wasn't the valedictorian, the straight-A student, or the standout in class. I was the regular one — the one who did just enough to get by. I stayed under the radar. I didn't push. I didn't stretch. I didn't want to stand out, because standing out meant attention — and attention was uncomfortable.

I had more in me, but I kept it tucked away, buried under layers of insecurity and fear. Fear of failing. Fear of being seen. Fear of trying hard and still not being enough. So, I coasted.

Not because I couldn't do more, but because I didn't believe I was **more**.

School was never hard for me, but it was never personal either. It felt like a routine — something I did, not something I embraced. I wasn't lazy, I was *unmoved*. And I thought average was enough for someone like me. Until one day, in an ordinary classroom, a teacher saw something **extraordinary** in me.

The Moment That Shifted My Mind

I remember that English class vividly. I had turned in yet another paper, written the night before - enough to get a grade, but not enough to matter. My teacher handed it back, paused, and looked me in the eyes with a kind of firmness that startled me.

She said, *"What if I graded you on your efforts to do better, not just the assignment? What would you make?* "I didn't know how to respond. No one had ever asked me that.

She wasn't asking about grammar or format. She was asking about **effort**.

About **intent**.

About the **choice** to try.

Then she said something that stayed with me for life: *"Try better. You are better than this."*

At the time, it didn't fully click. Her words were true, but I didn't have the confidence yet to act on them. I didn't see what she saw in me. But a seed was planted. And even if I didn't water it right away, it didn't die. Somewhere in me, I began to wonder... *What if she's right? What if I am better than this?*

What If I Am Better Than This?

For a long time, I questioned my worth. I let my current situation define me — the struggles, the rejections, the disappointments, the silent tears cried in the dark. My identity became entangled in what I lacked and what I failed to become in the eyes of others. I believed I was stuck, unworthy, and small. But what I didn't realize then was that my environment, my pain, and my temporary setbacks had distorted how I saw myself. I wasn't seeing clearly. I was measuring my value by my circumstances, not by the truth of who I was created to be. Somewhere along the way, I had forgotten how to dream. I silenced the voice that used to whisper, *"You were made for more."* Until now.

It was in the stillness, in a moment of quiet reflection, that a shift happened — a divine interruption. God reminded me of a dream I used to have as a child: flying above the sky, soaring past limitations, rising with ease. I used to believe I could do anything, be anything. And now I see that dream wasn't a fantasy — it was a prophecy. A glimpse into who I was always meant to be. I had allowed the weight of life to clip my wings, but those dreams were never lost, only buried. Now, they've been resurrected. The realization hit me like light breaking through the clouds: *What if I'm better than this?* Not better in pride or comparison — but better than the life of doubt, fear, and settling I had accepted. That question changed everything. I remembered that greatness was always in me, and that God never forgot.

Today, I walk differently. I speak differently. Because I know now that I *am* better than what I thought, better than the limits I placed on myself. I was created on purpose, for a purpose. Every battle refined me, every delay prepared me, every scar tells a story of survival. I am no longer defined by the valley — I'm shaped by it, but not confined to it. I am called to rise. I am choosing to believe again — to believe in the dreams God gave me, to believe in the strength He placed inside me, and to believe that my life still holds promise. I am not a victim of my past. I am the author of a new chapter. I'm not staying small. I'm flying again. Because *"they that wait upon the Lord shall renew their strength; they shall mount up with wings as eagles, they shall run and not be weary; they shall walk and not faint."* — Isaiah 40:31.

An Unexpected Door Opened

It wasn't academics that first rewarded me. It was **music.**

When I received a full scholarship in music, it changed how I saw myself. I didn't earn it because of my grades — I earned it because of my *gift*. And that scholarship was a reminder that **I had value**, even if I hadn't proven it on paper.

For the first time, I realized: *I don't have to be "like them" to be excellent. I just have to be me — fully.* That opportunity spoke a language I could finally hear: *You belong here. You can do this. You are not average. You are anointed.*

And yes, I still had insecurities. I still didn't think I was "academic material." But the door was open, and I walked through it. Hesitantly, at first. Quietly. **But I walked.**

And I didn't stop. What started as a music scholarship became the gateway to something I never imagined: **academic achievement.**

I started to push myself.

I started to study with intention.

I started to believe that *maybe* I was smart enough.

I started to fight for the "better" that teacher once spoke of.

And by the grace of God, I went on to earn not just one degree but **two bachelor's degrees, two master's degrees**, and even a **Ph.D.** I've received numerous **certifications** and continue to learn and grow. Not because I was the most gifted student, but because I was finally willing to believe something simple yet powerful: **"You don't have to be the best -just be your best."**

If you've ever said, *"I'm not smart enough,"* this chapter is for you. If you've ever sat in class and felt like everyone was ahead of you — this is for you.

If you've coasted, cruised, and convinced yourself that average was all you'd ever be — this is for you.

You are not disqualified.

You are not too late.

You are not too far behind.

There is **better** in you — and it's not about perfection. It's about *effort*. It's about showing up. It's about pushing past what you *feel* to walk into what you *are* capable of.

"I can do all things through Christ who strengthens me." – Philippians 4:13

I didn't think I could finish college. But I did - multiple times. I didn't think I was smart enough. But I was - I just had to try.

I didn't think I was worthy of excellence. But now I know: **God wired me for greatness — and He wired you too.**

It May Not Be College — But It Better Be Purpose

Let me be clear: a four-year college may not be your story. That's okay.

But **greatness must be.** Maybe your path is trade school, entrepreneurship, certifications, ministry, or creative arts — that doesn't make your journey any less powerful. Excellence isn't measured by diplomas; it's measured by obedience, effort, and vision.

Plan to be great.

In whatever lane you're called to — plan to dominate. Plan to be a master in your craft.

Plan to sharpen your mind.

Plan to build something that outlives you.

Don't let fear, insecurity, or past mistakes convince you that you aren't smart, capable, or worthy of more.

There Is an Angel Dispatched for You

I believe that God places **divine encouragers** in your life — people who are sent to wake up your potential. For me, it was that English teacher. She planted a sentence in my spirit that still echoes: *"Try better. You are better than this."*

God may be sending someone like that to you — or maybe *this chapter* is that voice for you right now. Whether it's a mentor, coach, parent, pastor, friend, or stranger, **there is an angel on assignment to push you into your better**. But here's the part many forget: **It's still your choice to move.**

You must decide that enough is enough. You must execute your better. You must put the plan into motion, even with shaking hands and a nervous heart. The enemy will whisper every reason why you're not enough. But God already declared why you are.

"Before I formed you in the womb, I knew you." – Jeremiah 1:5

You've been known.

You've been seen.

You've been appointed.

You were not created to live average. You were created for **impact**.

Try Better, Live Greater

So here's my challenge to you:

Stop coasting.

Stop hiding.

Stop waiting for someone to rescue your dreams.

Do better.

Live better.

Because **you are better than this.**

I was the kid who never thought college was for me. Now I stand with multiple degrees — not because I'm better than anyone, but because I finally believed I could be **better than who I was yesterday.** And if I can do it, **so can you.**

Better Awaits You - Go!

You may have been overlooked, underestimated, or even ignored — but that doesn't mean you're incapable. Just because you've coasted or played it small in the past doesn't mean greatness isn't inside of you. There comes a time when you must stop believing the lie that average is your ceiling. Whether your doubts came from your own insecurities or the silence of people who never spoke life into you, God has the final word — and His word says you are *capable, called,* and *complete in Him.* Better doesn't begin when you feel ready — it begins when you decide to try. Better happens when you silence the voice that says, "Who, me?" and answer boldly, "Yes, me." You were not made to merely survive life. You were made to show up, rise, and walk in the purpose that has been planted in you since the beginning.

Better awaits you, but it won't chase you. You have to move. You have to act. You have to do the uncomfortable thing and try harder than you did yesterday — not to prove anything to anyone else, but to honor the greatness God put in you. You may not take the traditional route. Your success may not come to be wrapped in degrees or diplomas, but that doesn't make it any less real. Excellence is about showing up, being intentional, and giving God your best — whatever "best" looks like in your lane. So rise. Plan for greatness. Execute your better. Because on the other side of obedience, effort, and faith is a life you never thought you were worthy of — but God always knew you were.

Don't let comparison rob you of your calling. My better is not your better, and your better isn't mine. We each have our own journey, our own struggles, our own timing, and our own assignment. Stop measuring your success against someone else's highlights. Better isn't about being on a stage, holding a title, or having degrees — better is about becoming who God *created* you to be. There is no competition in the Kingdom of God, only *completion*. When you compete, you chase approval. When you align, you walk in purpose. Know who you are. Know whose you are. And trust that **your better is already mapped out in the heart of God.**

You must align your better with **God's will** for your life. Ask Him, *"Lord, what does 'better' look like for me? Where are You taking me? What have You already placed inside me that I haven't activated yet?"* Get an understanding of His plan for you — not just what sounds good, but what's **God-ordained.** Success without direction is chaos, but when you understand your assignment, you stop chasing everything and start walking with clarity. Whether your path is in ministry, medicine, music, education, business, or something the world's never seen before — **walk boldly in it.** Stop asking for confirmation of what God already made clear: *you were made for more.*

So today, stop disqualifying yourself. Stop playing small. Stop trying to match a version of success that was never meant for you. The truth is, God's plan for your life is **not random — it's intentional, strategic, and victorious**. You're not just supposed to dream big, you're supposed to **live big** — in peace, in purpose, in excellence, and in wholeness. So step into your lane. Own your story. Chase your better. And know this: **God's version of better for you is not just possible — it's promised.**

My Prayer for BETTER

Lord, thank You for planting purpose in me, even when I couldn't see it. Thank You for the teachers, mentors, and voices that spoke life into me when I settled for less. For the one reading this who doubts their intelligence, their capacity, or their potential — stir up in them the courage to try better. Wake up every dormant dream. Silence every lie of inadequacy. And remind them that they are called to be excellent — not because of their background, but because of their design. May we no longer settle for average, but rise to the level of our anointing. In Jesus' name, Amen.

Scripture idea: *Proverbs 3:5-6 – "Trust in the Lord with all your heart... and He will make your paths straight."*

CHAPTER 4: GOD SEE YOU

Serving with a pure heart

From the earliest days, I watched my mother serve—quietly, humbly, sacrificially—I understood that true service is not a performance, but a posture of the heart. Her lesson, over the years, was this: service done from love and not obligation is sacred. When you serve right, you carry in your hands the fragrance of Christ, not the burdens of bitterness. But serving well is not always easy. You will face friction, disregard, or even direct hurt from those you sought to bless. These trials are not necessarily signs that your calling is wrong, but rather tests and refinements. Your task is to refuse to shrink; to preserve integrity—even when no one watches—and to continue blessing, knowing God sees the secret sacrifices.

Clean Hands, Pure Heart, Right Motive

Serving right starts with motive. You must ask yourself: *Why am I doing this?* Is it for recognition, return, or validation? Or is it simply because *this is who I am* — someone shaped by God to reflect His heart to others? The Scriptures call us to serve with a "pure heart" (1 Peter 1:22), and to keep "hands clean" (Psalm 24:3-4) so we may stand before God without shame. Outward acts are visible and valuable, but inner purity is what gives them eternal worth. You might do many good things, but if your heart carries strings—conditional love, hidden resentment—those acts become shadows. The enemy can't corrupt what begins in genuine devotion, but he will seduce what is built on compromise.

Serving Without Strings: Freedom over Contract

One of the most tender but difficult lessons is to serve without strings. Let your service not be bound by expectations, "if-then" agreements, or conditional attachment. When you serve with an invisible contract in your spirit—"if they love me back, I'll keep going"—you tether your heart to human circumstances. But true service flows from identity, not from response. You bless because that is your nature, shaped by the One who first loved you. In moments when people reject you, ignore you, or treat you as though you don't exist, those are invitations to deeper surrender. You choose to continue not because of them, but because of who God has made you to be.

Resilience in the Friction

This is a part of the journey. Just as metal must be rubbed to shine, your servant's heart will be tested by trials. Disrespect, neglect, misunderstanding, they will come. The call is not to shrink but to take root deeper. When friction comes, you have choices: respond in defensiveness, retreat, or stand with dignity. The last is hardest, but it is the posture of the higher way. If you allow offense to lead, you become reactive. But if you let grace govern your response, you show strength under pressure. Drawing from Christ's example—He served even when rejected—you continue in kindness, even when it costs you emotionally.

Keep Serving in the Hidden, Know God Sees

You may feel unseen. The cheered crowds may never gather. But serving faithfully in the hidden places is not lesser—it's honored in God's economy. Jesus taught that what is done in secret will be rewarded by the Father who sees in secret (Matthew 6:18). Keep doing the small acts of kindness, the silent prayers, the sacrificial giving. Your reward is not always on earth, but many times in heaven and in the deeper maturity your soul receives. When no one else knows, God knows. When your service costs you, God records it. Serve So That You Grow, Not So You Get. Your service should be transformational—for you and for others. It's not about accumulating recognition but about becoming more like Christ. Each act of humility, each small surrender, each moment you set aside your comfort for someone else, pieces of your character are refined. You learn patience, compassion, empathy, and grace. You begin to see the world beyond your narrow view, and your vision expands. The reward of serving is not always in what you receive, but in what you become.

Let Trials Shape, Not Break

Your trial is not the enemy of your purpose—they are the soil where purpose grows. What once felt like a wound or injustice can become a wellspring of empathy, authority, and depth. The things you endured equip you to minister to others who walk similar paths. You gain credibility not because you avoided storms, but because you navigated them. God uses your past to position you. So, allow your trials to shape you—to sharpen your character, deepen your faith, and widen your capacity for genuine compassion. You don't carry bitterness, you carry testimony.

Remember the Eternal Audience

People's approval is fleeting; God's approval is eternal. Serve knowing that your highest applause is from Heaven. Let's not forget that many biblical heroes served and were misunderstood, mocked, or marginalized in their time. Yet their legacy stands. You are working not for the temporal, but for the eternal. Let your eyes fix on the eternal audience, and let that perspective guard your heart from discouraged retreat.

When applause dies, souls remain touched. What you sow in faith bears fruit beyond your sight.

You don't need grand gestures or perfect conditions. Sometimes, simply showing kindness, helping someone in need, or being present matters more. Serve by listening. Serve by giving. Serve by encouraging. Serving with integrity means doing the right thing even when no one is watching, even when praise doesn't come. Clean hands. Clean heart. Your motive matters. Colossians 3:23-24 says, *"Whatever you do, work at it with all your heart, as working for the Lord, not for human masters… It is the Lord Christ you are serving."* This reminds us that our service isn't ultimately about people's approval—it's about honoring God. Having integrity also means consistency. It means showing up even when it's hard, doing what's right even when it costs. God honors that kind of faithfulness even more than visible success.

When you serve with a clean heart, no hidden expectations - you reflect Christ. When you serve because of God, your life becomes a blessing to others, and in serving them, you grow closer to the heart of God.

CHAPTER 5: THE O ZONE- OCCUPYING THE ZONE OF OPPORTUNITY

Workplace injustice, standing for truth, and spiritual warfare.

The **O-Zone** is not just the layer of the atmosphere — it's the **Zone of Opportunity**. It's your career, your business, your ministry, your role in the community — **any space where you serve, grow, and show up with purpose**. It's the place where your gift meets responsibility, where your anointing is tested, and where favor puts you in rooms your résumé can't always explain. But just like the atmosphere, the O-Zone can come under attack. And for many of us, especially those walking in integrity and spiritual authority, **the battlefield isn't just personal — it's professional.**

I worked for a large, well-known company for many years. I gave it my best. I showed up on time, went the extra mile, helped others, and did my job with excellence. Like many of you, I didn't clock in just to get a paycheck — I served as unto the Lord. I believed in doing right. I believed in giving people grace. I believed in showing love, even when it wasn't returned. But what I didn't expect was the **politics, power struggles,**

and petty sabotage that hid behind smiling faces and so-called teamwork.

Some people aren't threatened by their skill — they're threatened by your **favor**. Your integrity shines a light on their compromise. Your consistency exposes their laziness. Your influence draws people, not because you're trying, but because God put a light in you that *can't be dimmed*. And for some, that's too much.

When Favor Feels Like a Target

A young lady who started and appeared to be a great team leader. She was smart, polished, well-spoken, and if you did not surpass her in position, strategy, or promotion, she was just fine — at least on the surface. I honestly felt that this was a great opportunity and honored her leadership. But as I started to **climb the ladder**, receiving new assignments and recognition, something shifted. Her compliments grew cold. Her support disappeared. And her eyes started to watch me - not with mentorship, but with **monitoring**. Have you ever felt someone smile at you, but you knew - deep down, she was rooting for your fall? As my work began to receive attention from upper leadership, her behavior became more strategic. Meetings I wasn't invited to. Emails I wasn't copied on. Projects I had been leading were quietly reassigned. At first, I second-guessed myself. *Maybe I'm overthinking this. Maybe I'm too sensitive.* But eventually, the truth came to light: she was building a case that was not purposed for my success.

When Respect Meets Betrayal — But God Steps In

I respected her. I admired her leadership. I was genuinely grateful for the opportunity to work alongside this woman. I supported her vision, honored her position, and gave my best. Never in my mind did I imagine that behind the scenes, she was plotting my termination. The same person whose leadership I celebrated was quietly orchestrating my removal. That realization was painful. Betrayal always is. It cuts deep because it comes from those you trusted, those you thought were on your side. But even in that dark moment, I saw God's hand moving.

What she planned in secret, God exposed in the open. What was meant to harm me, God used to elevate and protect me. Instead of losing everything, I was preserved. Instead of being humiliated, I was honored. God raised others — even leaders at higher levels — to step in on my behalf. They corrected the paperwork, ensured I received the retirement and benefits I had rightfully earned, and reversed the outcome she had intended. That wasn't a coincidence. That was *divine intervention.*

That was God saying, "You don't have to fight this battle. I've already won it for you."

This experience reminded me that my life is not at the mercy of human plots or decisions. God is my protector, my advocate, and my vindicator. Even when I can't see what's happening, He is at work. And when you know who you are in Christ, you don't have to fear betrayal or manipulation. You can serve with integrity, forgive even when it hurts, and trust that God's justice will prevail. In the end, I walked away not bitter but blessed. Because as the Word says, **"No weapon formed against you shall prosper, and every tongue that rises against you in judgment you shall condemn. This is the heritage of the servants of the Lord, and their righteousness is from Me, says the Lord."** — *Isaiah 54:17*

When God Sends Favor from the Top

There are moments in life when the battle feels unjust — when lies are spoken, decisions are made in darkness, and it seems like you're being pushed out without cause. That was my reality. A manager made a decision to remove me, not based on truth or performance, but through manipulation and falsehood. It felt like a betrayal. I had served with integrity, shown up with excellence, and still, I was being discarded. But just when it looked like the enemy would win, *God stepped in.*

God didn't just defend me quietly — He sent help from the top. A Senior Vice President, someone who had every reason to stay distant, came off of sick leave — not for their own gain, but to make sure the paperwork told *the truth*. To ensure that my exit reflected the honor, years, and dedication I had poured into it. Retirement, not removal. Full financial recognition, not stripped benefits. That's what favor looks like. That's what it means when God says, *"I will prepare a table before you in the presence of your enemies."* I didn't have to fight or force anything. I kept serving, kept working as if unto the Lord, and God fought the battle for me. He brought justice in a way only He can.

It was hard — deeply painful at times — but I never forgot who I was. And more importantly, *who* I was. In Christ, I am not forgotten. I am not at the mercy of man. I am seen, protected, and favored. When you know who you are in Christ, you stop reacting out of fear and start walking in authority. You realize that no weapon formed against you will prosper. You don't have to chase revenge — just stay faithful, and God will take care of everything. In the end, victory wasn't just possible — it was promised. As it is written: **"And we know that in all things God works for the good of those who love Him, who have been called according to His purpose."** — *Romans 8:28*

The Plot that Failed!!!

After **years of faithful service**, I was told I would be **terminated** — and it was based on her recommendation. No formal warnings. No poor performance reviews. Just an internal decision, based on influenced by someone who couldn't handle my favor. They couldn't fire me for cause, so they tried to **silence my contribution**, erase my value, and remove me quietly.

But here's the part they forgot: **You can't fire what God hired.**

God never promised that the road would be fair — but He did promise that **what He starts, He finishes.** When He places you in the O-Zone, your zone of opportunity — He doesn't need man's permission to keep you there. Favor doesn't expire because of office politics. Destiny isn't voted on in HR meetings. I was heartbroken, frustrated, and stunned — but I didn't lash out. I didn't retaliate. I didn't stoop to the level of sabotage. Instead, **I held on to integrity**, and I **let God be my defense**. And let me tell you — **God made it right.**

The workplace can be one of the **greatest testing grounds** for your character. It's easy to be kind when people are kind back. But what about when they slander your name? What about when they smile in your face and stab you in your absence? What about when you're the one training the person who got promoted over you?

It's in those moments that the **real you is revealed**. And I made a decision early on: I would not let *anyone* cause me to step out of character or compromise my calling.

"The Lord will fight for you; you need only to be still." – Exodus 14:14

Being still doesn't mean being passive. It means **moving in obedience**, not offense. It means staying excellent, even when others are evil. It means praying for your enemies while they plan your downfall. Because when you serve with integrity in your O-Zone, **God will make the crooked places straight**.

The Enemy Became My Stepladder

Here's the part I need you to catch: The same people who tried to push me down ended up **elevating me**. That false report didn't end my career — it **propelled** it. What was meant for harm became my stepping stone. God used the exposure to *reposition* me, *rebuild* me, and *reveal* just how **unshakeable** His hand is on my life.

Instead of being terminated, I was **transitioned** into a greater opportunity. Instead of being removed, I was **reassigned with**

purpose. God used that season to remind me: **Your destiny is not determined by titles, managers, or man-made structures. It is sustained by obedience and protected by grace.**

One of the greatest victories you will ever walk in is the ability to **release those who tried to ruin you**. Don't carry grudges or allow hate to poison your heart. Bitterness will only slow your elevation. Instead, **pray for them**. Love them, even from a distance. Not because they were right — but because you refuse to let their actions define your future. The **law of reciprocity** is real: what a person sows, they will surely reap. You don't have to seek revenge or fight dirty — **God is your battle strategist**, and He never loses a war. The same grace that sustained you will deal with every hidden agenda, every false accusation, and every backroom conversation meant to stop you. Stay the course. Keep your heart pure. Keep your vision clear. And most of all, **continue to soar with purpose**, knowing that those who rise above don't flap in chaos — they glide on God's wind.

There is a special kind of strength that comes when you realize your enemies — especially those in the workplace — were not placed in your life to destroy you but to **develop you**. I now see clearly that the very people who tried to block my promotion, silence my contributions, and tarnish my name were unknowingly used by God to **push me into purpose**. Their attacks became my training ground. Their resistance became my stretching place. And what they meant to bury me only **planted me deeper into destiny**.

Yes, the enemy at work became my **stepping stool to excellence and progression**. Every time they lied, I grew stronger. Every time they conspired, I prayed harder. Every door they tried to close, God opened a bigger one. Their rejection redirected me into the right rooms, with the right people, for the right reasons. And eventually, I stood in positions of influence they never wanted me to reach — not through manipulation or backdoor deals, but through **God's undeniable favor** and my consistent integrity.

But here's the test many fail: *How do you treat the people who are now under your feet?*

When you've climbed the ladder and those same individuals who once tried to sabotage you now need your approval, your leadership, or your influence — it is tempting to return what they gave you. But I chose differently. I chose not to abuse them, belittle them, or remind them of what they did. Why? Because **vindication doesn't require vengeance**. Just because someone is now beneath you doesn't mean you become what they were to you. **Elevation is not a license to retaliate — it's an opportunity to reveal your maturity.**

I've learned that holding on to bitterness, even with a justified reason, only poisons your progress. When you refuse to let go, you chain yourself to the offense — and how can you run free when you're still dragging the weight of the past? I decided: **I will not be bound by resentment.** I don't need to see them fall. I don't need to remind them of who I've become. Their actions are between them and God. But as for me, I will rise **without compromising my character.**

The truth is, when God truly elevates you, it humbles you. You realize that your platform is not just for celebration — it's for stewardship. So I lead with grace. I serve with humility. And I remember that if He placed me above, it was never to look down on anyone, but to **lift others as I climb**. The enemy thought they were burying me — but God was simply building a foundation for something greater. And now, I stand firm, not in pride, but in purpose. **Because of them, I went higher — but because of Him, I stayed whole.**

Encouragement for the Workplace Warrior

To you, the one who's reading this while working in an environment where you feel unseen or unfairly treated is for you.

You might be doing everything right and still feel like the enemy is working overtime to wear you down. You may be pouring your all into your career, and yet someone in leadership is trying to dim your light. But hear me clearly:

- God sees you.
- God knows your heart.
- God honors integrity.
- God will vindicate you.

Don't allow workplace warfare to cause you to misrepresent your witness. **Serve with excellence. Speak with wisdom. Move with purpose.** Keep giving your best, not for man's approval, but as a reflection of the One who sent you into that zone in the first place.

"Whatever you do, work at it with all your heart, as working for the Lord, not for human masters." – Colossians 3:23

God didn't place you in your career by accident. You are called to occupy the zone. The **O-Zone** is where your anointing and assignment collide. It's where your faith must be strong and your fruit must be visible. Yes, people will come against you. Yes, favor will feel like a threat to those who walk in fear. But you don't have to fear them — you walk with the **Author of Promotion.**

The enemy cannot close a door God has ordained. And even if one door shuts, He will open another that no man can block. The workplace is not just a paycheck — it's a platform. A stage where you live out what you preach. A test of who you are when things get tight. A place where God gets the glory, *even when man tries to take the credit.*

You are a beacon of light, uniquely created by God, and that light cannot be dimmed. In Matthew 5:14-16, Jesus calls us the "light of the world," and He encourages us to let our light shine before others, so they may see our good works and glorify our Father in heaven. This light within you is not meant to be hidden or suppressed, even when others may not understand or feel threatened by it. You were designed to shine with purpose and grace, and in doing so, you bring glory to God and inspire others. Do not dim your light out of fear of making others uncomfortable, for your brilliance is a reflection of God's greatness.

When others' insecurities try to project onto you, remember that their limitations are not your own. In 2 Timothy 1:7, it is written, "For God gave us a spirit not of fear but of power and love and self-control." Fear is often rooted in the insecurity and jealousy of others, and it's important to recognize that their struggles do not define your worth. Your confidence in Christ should remain unshaken, and when you rise, you allow others to rise with you. Shine with the love and power that God has instilled in you—doing so helps break down barriers and opens doors for others to embrace their own light.

Never be afraid to soar, because your blessings are meant to flow outward, touching the lives of those around you. Psalm 139:14 declares, "I praise you because I am fearfully and wonderfully made," and this truth is your foundation. You are fearfully and wonderfully made to do incredible things for God's kingdom. Each step you take, every act of kindness, every moment of strength, is a testament to the goodness of God in you. When you soar in faith, others will be blessed by your testimony, and God's glory will be revealed through your actions. Continue to rise and shine without hesitation, because the world needs the light that only you can provide.

Moving forward with confidence in who God has created you to be is not only a blessing to yourself but a powerful way to impact the lives of others. In Philippians 3:13-14, Paul encourages us to "forget what is behind and strain toward what is ahead." This means that regardless of past struggles, doubts, or challenges, we are called to press forward with purpose and to celebrate the unique person God has shaped us to be. Embrace your journey, understanding that each step forward is a step in fulfilling God's plan for you, a plan that will bless others through your actions, words, and presence.

Celebrating yourself is not an act of arrogance but a recognition of God's faithfulness in your life. When you celebrate who you are, you honor the Creator who designed you with love, intention, and grace. Psalm 118:24 reminds us that "This is the day the Lord has made; let us rejoice and be glad in it." Rejoicing in yourself is an acknowledgment that you are fearfully and wonderfully made. As you stand tall in your identity, free from the constraints of comparison or insecurity, you radiate that joy and peace to those around you. The more you celebrate your unique gifts and qualities, the more you encourage others to do the same, creating an environment of mutual support, growth, and encouragement.

As you move forward in this journey, you become a living testament to God's goodness, and your life becomes a blessing to others. Jesus calls us to love our neighbors as ourselves (Mark 12:31), and part of loving others well is first learning to love and appreciate ourselves in the way God intended. When you move forward with purpose, embracing the fullness of who you are, you make space for others to step into their own greatness. Your journey of growth, empowerment, and celebration becomes a catalyst for the growth of those around you. So move forward confidently, celebrate your progress, and know that in doing so, you are shining a light that encourages and uplifts the world around you.

Stay in Position, Victory Is Certain

So, to every dreamer, every hard worker, every kingdom-minded leader — **don't move out of position.** Don't let betrayal make you bitter. Don't let sabotage make you small. Don't let their plans shake your purpose. **Stay faithful. Stay focused. Stay fruitful.**

God is your source. The O-Zone is your assignment. And the enemy — though he plots — will always be outmatched by the One who called you. **"You can't be fired from what Heaven hired you for'**

One of the greatest victories you will ever walk in is the ability to **release those who tried to ruin you**. Don't carry grudges or allow hate to poison your heart. Bitterness will only slow your elevation. Instead, **pray for them**. Love them, even from a distance. Not because they were right — but because you refuse to let their actions define your future. The **law of reciprocity** is real: what a person sows, they will surely reap. You don't have to seek revenge or fight dirty — **God is your battle strategist**, and He never loses a war. The same grace that sustained you will deal with every hidden agenda, every false accusation, and every backroom conversation meant to stop you. Stay the course. Keep your heart pure. Keep your vision clear. And most of all, **continue to soar with purpose**, knowing that those who rise above don't flap in chaos -**they glide on God's wind.**

I will not be moved by fear, politics, or pressure. I was chosen for this zone, and I will serve with boldness, integrity, and faith. God is my defender, my promoter, and my provider. I declare that no weapon formed against me shall prosper, and every tongue that rises against me in judgment shall be condemned. I don't work for man's applause — I work for God's glory. I occupy the zone of opportunity with excellence, and I trust that what God started in me, He will surely complete. In Jesus' name, Amen.

Scripture idea: *Isaiah 54:17 – "No weapon formed against you shall prosper..."*

CHAPTER 6: LOVE IS NOT LOVE UNTIL YOU LOVE!

What I've Learned in the process

I thought I knew what love was. Fresh out of high school, stepping into my first year of college, I decided to get married -young, hopeful, and full of dreams. I had never truly seen love modeled well, but I believed in it. I believed in the idea of forever. I believed that choosing to marry meant choosing something safe, solid, and secure. I thought it meant stability. Belonging, A forever place. But here's what I learned the hard way: **when a relationship is not ordained by God, it is not safe, solid, or secure,** no matter how good the intentions are. In fact, it can be the complete opposite. It can be unstable. Confusing. Painful. Even destructive.

Why I Now Believe in Waiting on God :

1. **God Sees What You Don't.**

    You may be in love, but God sees the heart, the future, the spiritual condition, and the hidden things. When you wait on Him, He'll protect you from what looks good but is not *God*.

2. **Your Purpose Comes Before the Partnership:** You need time to discover who you are in Christ. Know your calling. Walk-in healing. Understand your voice. Marriage should complement your purpose - not become a detour from it.

3. **Time Reveals Truth:** People can only pretend for so long. Time reveals character, habits, maturity, faithfulness, and values. When you rush, you marry the image. When you wait, you meet reality.

4. **Preparation Prevents Heartbreak:** A wedding takes a day. Marriage takes a lifetime. Take time to grow spiritually, emotionally, and mentally. Talk about finances, healing, communication, and purpose *before* you say "I do."

5. **Peace Is a Confirmation:** If you have to force it, fear it, or fake it — it's not from God. His presence brings peace. His will won't leave you confused. Waiting on Him leads to rest, not anxiety.

Capacity vs. Compatibility: Understanding Love's Limits

One of the hardest truths to accept in life is this: **People can only love you according to their capacity -not your expectations.**

Someone may care deeply, but if they've never learned *healthy love,* if they've never been healed, if they were never taught how to communicate, be present, show empathy, or make sacrifices - then their version of love will reflect that *limited capacity*. It's not always that they don't love you... It's that they don't know *how* to love you in a way that's healthy, whole, or God-aligned. And here's the hard part:

Their limited love may still hurt you.

Because while they're giving what they *can,* it still may not be what you *need.* You can end up feeling neglected, frustrated, unseen -not because they're intentionally trying to wound you, but because they're loving you with a version of love that's incomplete, underdeveloped, or broken.

This is why discernment is so important — especially in relationships and marriage. Because **it's not just about whether someone loves you... It's about whether their love is *compatible* with your heart, your values, and your emotional and spiritual needs.**

God's love is the only perfect love. Human love is always filtered through experience, wounds, beliefs, and growth. That's why you must:

- Know your worth before seeking love,
- Know your needs before settling for attention,
- Know your purpose before tying your life to someone else's patterns.

What do you do with this truth?

1. **Stop personalizing someone's inability to love you well.** Their limits are not your fault.
2. **Acknowledge when love feels like pain — and don't romanticize it.** God never called you to stay in dysfunction disguised as devotion.
3. **Be honest about your needs.** It's not selfish to want emotional safety, consistency, respect, and peace.
4. **Choose partners, friends, and even mentors based on spiritual maturity, not just emotional intensity.**
5. **Let God love you first.** He sets the standard. He fills the void. And when you're filled with His love, you stop trying to bleed for those who were never meant to hold your heart in the first place.

What I understand now is that **love is not just a feeling — it's a foundation.** And if that foundation is cracked, unstable, or built on broken promises, the whole structure will eventually fall. I knew going in that he struggled with commitment. I saw the signs, but I wanted to believe that love — or my love — could fix it. That would be enough. But the truth is, love cannot carry what only healing, maturity, and surrender to God can fix.

I lost parts of myself trying to hold up something that wasn't mine to hold alone. But *God.* He stepped in and **rescued me — not just from the relationship, but from the lie that I wasn't worthy of real love.** He spared my life, emotionally and spiritually. And in the ruins of that early marriage, He began rebuilding *me.*

I survived. And not just barely -I came out stronger, wiser, and more *sure of myself.* I learned that **love is not a game.** It's not something to rush into, and it's not a bandage for brokenness. **Love is sacred. Love is a covenant. Love is truth.** And while what I went through hurt me deeply, it also healed me in ways I didn't know I needed. It showed me how to set boundaries. It taught me how to listen to red flags. It pushed me closer to God, who is the only One who loves perfectly.

So to anyone who thinks love is supposed to hurt, *it's not.* To anyone rushing into love to escape something else -*slow down.* And to anyone who's been through it, who's barely made it out - *you're not alone, and you're not broken.* You survived, and survival is the seed of purpose.

The Mirror that saved me

Not just the glass hanging on the wall, but the deeper reflection it demanded I see. For a long time, I blamed others for my pain, my choices, and my circumstances. I thought if they had treated me better, if life had been kinder, then I would've been happier, more whole. But one day, I stood in front of the mirror and saw someone who was still waiting to be chosen… by *themselves*. That's when it hit me: *love and life are a choice.* And the first person I had to choose was *me*. No more pointing fingers. No more waiting. I had to decide that I was worth loving, worth changing for, and worth showing up for.

Looking in the mirror—physically and spiritually—is a bold act. It's easy to look at others, but it takes courage to look at *yourself* with honesty. James 1:23-24 talks about those who hear the word and don't do it as being like someone who looks at themselves in a mirror and forgets what they look like. The mirror is not just a place of reflection—it's a place of *revelation*. You have to look beyond the surface, beyond the pain, beyond the masks, and see the truth. Who am I *really*? What wounds am I still carrying? What lies have I believed about myself? What greatness have I been afraid to step into? When you face yourself truthfully, you begin the real work of healing and transformation.

Loving yourself doesn't mean being perfect—it means embracing the truth of who God made you to be. It means seeing yourself through *His* eyes, not through the eyes of people who didn't understand your value. Psalm 139:14 says, *"I praise You because I am fearfully and wonderfully made; Your works are wonderful, I know that full well."* That scripture isn't just a beautiful verse—it's a mirror. It reflects to you your divine design. When you really believe that God made you with intention, you stop waiting for others to validate your worth. You begin to *value yourself.* And from that place, love no longer feels like a struggle—it becomes natural.

The moment you identify who *you* are—your worth, your voice, your purpose—that's when everything changes. You realize no one else is responsible for your healing. No one else can make you love yourself. You must say to the person in the mirror, *"It is ME who must make the change. It is ME who must rise. It is ME who must stop running from my own reflection."* And when you do, freedom begins. You stop living by fear and start living by truth. You stop shrinking and start standing tall. You stop existing and start *living.* Fully. Authentically. Boldly.

Go to the mirror—not just to fix your hair or adjust your clothes—but to *see yourself.* Speak life to the reflection staring back at you. Tell yourself, "I choose you. I love you. I believe in you." Choose to do the work. Choose to love you like God loves you—unconditionally, graciously, and consistently. The mirror can't lie, but it can reveal. And once you really *see* you, no one can unsee your worth again.

When you finally *see yourself*—truly, deeply—you begin a healing that no one else can do for you. The reflection staring back at you in the mirror is more than just skin and features; it's your story, your battles, your becoming. That reflection is *you*—the you who has been through heartbreak and disappointment, the you who has survived silent struggles and still showed up. And instead of judging or criticizing that image, it's time to speak life to it. Say it out loud: *"I choose you. I love you. I believe in you."* Those aren't just affirmations—they're declarations of ownership, of accountability, of love. Because when you choose yourself, you give yourself permission to grow, to heal, and to love others in a healthy, whole way.

Choosing you is not selfish—it's *sacred*. It's saying, "I am no longer waiting for someone else to fix me, approve of me, or save me." When you choose yourself, you begin to make room for peace, for growth, and for transformation. You no longer resist change—you invite it. You begin to understand that every version of you deserves compassion: the past you, the healing you, and the becoming you. And from that awareness, you stop expecting others to give what you have now chosen to give yourself—love, acceptance, and grace. You begin to hold yourself accountable not with shame, but with mercy. That's where true transformation begins.

When you've truly seen yourself and chosen love, you become better equipped to love others the way God calls us to—with *agape love*. That's the kind of love that is unconditional, patient, and not rooted in performance. But here's the key: you can't give agape love if you haven't received it—from God *and* from yourself. When you choose yourself, you no longer project your pain onto people. You no longer take offense personally or live guarded by fear. You can deal with people gently, with understanding, because you've done the inner work of loving the reflection in the mirror. The love you show others becomes a reflection of the love you've cultivated within.

Stand in the mirror-not with shame, but with reverence. Look at the reflection and say, *"It's me. It's always been me. And now, I choose me."* That choice is your turning point. It's your foundation. And from there, love flows more freely, peace becomes your default, and purpose begins to take shape. You begin to love right because you're no longer loving from emptiness—you're loving from overflow. The reflection in the mirror is not just someone who made it through; it's someone who decided to live fully, love deeply, and walk boldly. And that—*that* is power. That's the beginning of true love—when it starts with *you*.

You are *loved*- a truth so deep and transformative that it can change the very core of who you are. In moments of despair, when everything else seems to fail, love remains the constant, unshakable force that lifts us from the depths of our struggles. 1 Corinthians 13:7 tells us that love "bears all things, believes all things, hopes all things, endures all things." Love, as shown through God's grace, is the lifter that holds us up when we are weak. It doesn't falter, doesn't fail, and it always has the power to lift us higher, reminding us that no matter what the circumstances, we are never alone. God's love is a sure foundation that can carry us through any storm.

However, to fully experience the transformative power of love, we must first understand what love truly looks and feels like. Too often, the world distorts love, equating it with fleeting emotions or conditional affection. But God's love is unconditional, unchanging, and perfect. In 1 John 4:9-10, it is written: "This is how God showed his love among us: He sent his one and only Son into the world that we might live through him. This is love: not that we loved God, but that he loved us and sent his Son as an atoning sacrifice for our sins." God's love is sacrificial, selfless, and it doesn't require us to be perfect. When we receive this love in its purest form, we begin to understand that it's not about what we do, but about who God is and how He sees us.

Receiving God's love is the foundation that enables us to pass His love on to others. When we grasp the depth of God's love for us, we are empowered to reflect that love outwardly. Jesus taught us to love one another as He has loved us (John 13:34), and by accepting His love, we can give that same love to others. Love is not just an emotion; it's an action. It's being present, offering grace, speaking kindness, and showing compassion. By allowing God's love to fill our hearts, we become vessels of His love, passing it along to others in tangible ways. And as we share His love, it becomes a cycle of healing, encouragement, and growth, reminding us all that we are never beyond the reach of God's perfect love.

CHAPTER 7: EAGLE WINGS... EAGLE VISION

The Bible uses the eagle as a symbol of divine strength and perspective. Isaiah 40:31 says, *"But those who hope in the Lord will renew their strength. They will soar on wings like eagles; they will run and not grow weary..."* That verse became real to me, not just in theory, but in my spirit. Eagles rise above storms. While other birds hide, the eagle soars into the wind and lets the storm lift it higher. That's what God was doing for me. My home life was a storm, but in the middle of it, God was lifting me above it, giving me vision and hope that my story would not end in pain.

There is something deeply symbolic and spiritually rich about the eagle. Long before I understood the full weight of your father's words, even in his brokenness, he was planting seeds of wisdom. When he sang about *"the eagle stirring its nest,"* he was drawing from a powerful biblical image found in Deuteronomy 32:11: *"Like an eagle that stirs up its nest and hovers over its young, that spreads its wings to catch them and carries them aloft."* Whether he knew it or not in the moment, he was teaching you something divine—about growth, discomfort, strength, and vision. The eagle is one of the most majestic and fearless creatures in all of nature. It has unmatched vision—able to see miles ahead with clarity and focus. This represents foresight and purpose. Just like the eagle, you are called to rise above the distractions and limitations of the earth, to see beyond the temporary and focus on the eternal. Isaiah 40:31 declares, *"But those who wait on the Lord shall renew their strength; they shall mount up with wings like eagles."* This isn't just poetic—it's prophetic. God has equipped you with vision, with strength, and with wings to soar far above fear, failure, and doubt.

When an eagle stirs its nest, it is intentionally making the space uncomfortable for its young. The soft feathers and comfort are removed so the eaglets are forced to learn to fly. It's not cruelty—it's preparation. In the same way, life may push you out of comfort zones, shake your security, and even leave you wondering why things had to change. But the stirring is divine. It's not meant to break you—it's meant to build your wings. God, like that mother eagle, is calling you higher, and He knows that staying in the nest too long will keep you grounded. You were never meant to stay low—you were created to *soar*.

My father, even in his most human and imperfect state, was prophesying about my future. He saw something powerful in the eagle-and something powerful in *me*. Whether he could express it clearly or not, his spirit understood the call to rise above. He saw the stirring not just as chaos, but as a call to strength. And now, you get to carry that legacy forward—not as a memory of pain, but as a revelation of power. So, embrace the eagle within you. Embrace the stirring, the discomfort, the challenge. You are being called to higher ground, to sharper vision, to stronger wings. You are not meant to dwell among chickens pecking at the ground—you were born to ride the wind, to see far, and to lead with purpose. Let the cry of the eagle rise from within you. Lift your head, spread your wings, and *soar*-not just for yourself, but for everyone who is still in the nest, waiting for someone to show them that flying is possible.

My prayer is that you find the strength to rise above it all — the hurt, the disappointments, the setbacks, the silent battles, the weariness. That you rise like the **eagle**, high above the storm. Because the truth is, eagles are *built* for storms. While other birds hide from the wind and rain, the eagle flies *into* the storm -not to suffer in it, but to **use it**.

The storm's wind actually lifts the eagle higher. It locks its wings, stretches them wide, and lets the turbulence push it to altitudes it could never reach on its own. Isn't that just like God? The very thing that was meant to bring you down, He'll use to lift you— if you don't quit. If you trust Him in the storm.

But it's not just the wings that make the eagle powerful — it's the **vision**.

The eagle's eyesight is *five times* stronger than the average human's. An eagle can see another eagle soaring miles away — and it can spot its target from over two miles in the sky. Its **vision is focused, sharp, and undistracted.** The eagle doesn't flap wildly or waste energy. It locks in, waits for the right moment, and then *moves with precision*. That's how I want you to rise with vision. Don't let distractions blur your purpose. Don't let temporary pain distort your perspective. Ask God to give you eagle-eyed faith: to see beyond the moment, to rise above the noise, and to lock into your calling. In life, distractions are constant noise from the world, doubts in the mind, and storms of circumstance that try to knock us off course. But if you want to walk in purpose and victory, you must develop the *mindset of an eagle*. The eagle is not just a symbol of strength; it is a masterclass in focus, discipline, and strategy. It doesn't get distracted by every movement around it. It doesn't waste energy on things beneath it. The eagle rises above. And so must you.

An eagle soars higher than any other bird. It has the ability to fly up to altitudes of 10,000 feet, yet when it spots its prey, it can dive at speeds over 100 miles per hour with laser-sharp focus. That's the type of clarity and determination God wants you to walk in. Isaiah 40:31 says, *"But they that wait upon the Lord shall renew their strength; they shall mount up with wings as eagles…"*

This verse isn't just about physical strength; it's about rising in spirit, in vision, and in faith. Eagles don't flap frantically like other birds; they soar, carried by the wind. Likewise, when you wait on the Lord, when you align with His will, you won't have to strive in your own strength; you'll rise by His Spirit.

The Rise: Above Distraction and Into Purpose

To rise like an eagle, you must first recognize what weighs you down. Distractions can come in many forms—comparison, fear, people-pleasing, even comfort. Eagles do not mingle with flocks of pigeons or sparrows. They fly alone, not because they are lonely, but because they are focused. Some people are not meant to go where you're going. Some conversations are too small for your destiny. Some battles are not worth your energy. The eagle's rise begins with separation—choosing to walk a higher path, think higher thoughts, and pursue a higher calling.

Purpose requires discipline. The eagle doesn't just fly aimlessly; it rises with intention. God has placed purpose inside of you, but it requires vision to pursue it. Like the eagle, you must train your eyes to see beyond the surface, to spot opportunities and threats with discernment. Proverbs 29:18 says, *"Where there is no vision, the people perish."* If you allow distractions to blur your vision, you will never reach the heights God intended. But when your eyes are fixed on what He has called you to, nothing can pull you off track. One of the most powerful things about the eagle is how it handles storms. While most birds run for cover when a storm approaches, the eagle *flies toward it*. It uses the wind and turbulence of the storm to lift itself *higher*. The very thing that causes others to retreat, the eagle uses to advance. That's not just instinct—that's strategy. That's resilience. And that's the mindset you need to develop.

Storms in life are inevitable—loss, failure, betrayal, disappointment. But storms are not signs of weakness; they are opportunities for elevation. James 1:2-4 tells us to *"count it all joy when you fall into various trials, knowing that the testing of your faith produces endurance."* God uses storms to strengthen your wings, to stretch your faith, and to shift your position. When you face adversity with the eagle's mindset, you no longer fear the storm—you *rise* because of it.

The eagle wins because it understands the storm is part of the journey. It doesn't panic; it positions. You, too, must learn to position yourself when trials come—not in fear, but in faith. Stand firm. Set your eyes on what's above. Know that God is not asking you to escape the storm—He's empowering you to *rise through it*.

Becoming the Eagle

To adopt the eagle's mindset is to make a daily choice: to rise, to focus, to believe, and to endure. It means refusing to settle for the ground when you were made for the sky. It means recognizing that you are not defined by what's around you, but by what's *within* you—by what God has placed in your spirit.

Like an eagle, you must:

- *Separate* yourself from the noise.
- *Sharpen* your vision through prayer and the Word.
- *Soar* with purpose, not panic.
- *Stretch* your wings in faith when the winds of adversity blow.

Let every distraction be a reminder to refocus. Let every storm be a launching pad, not a limitation. And let every setback push you to go *higher* in God.

The eagle doesn't ask the storm to stop-it just flies above it. That's your call, too. Not to beg for easy days, but to grow stronger wings. Not to shrink in fear, but to soar in faith. Because when your heart is set on purpose, and your mind is anchored in truth, *nothing*—not fear, not failure, not distraction—can hold you down. Keep your eyes fixed above. And soar into the purpose God designed just for you.

Because you *can* rise above it all, you were never meant to live grounded by fear, shame, or brokenness. You were created to *soar*. *RISE and SOAR!*

"But they that wait upon the Lord shall renew their strength; they shall mount up with wings as eagles; they shall run and not be weary; they shall walk and not faint." — *Isaiah 40:31*

Rising Above: How God Revealed My Purpose Through Dreams

From my earliest years, even in the middle of my most painful and frightening moments, I sensed that my life was not an accident. I say this not out of arrogance, but out of deep reverence and gratitude: I am sure that God purposed my life. This certainty didn't arrive all at once; it was revealed slowly, like sunlight breaking through a storm. While I endured abuse, trauma, and distress, God was already planting seeds of hope inside me. He was speaking to me in ways I could understand as a child — most powerfully through my dreams. Those dreams became lifelines, messages of love and reassurance from a God who saw me when others overlooked me, who spoke when others silenced me.

One of the clearest ways God spoke to me was through dreams of flying. In the scariest and darkest seasons of my life, I would dream of my body rising, soaring with the magnitude and strength of an aircraft. In these dreams, I could look down and see myself — the child in pain, mistreated, scared, and struggling — but my spirit was rising above it all. This wasn't escapism. It was a revelation. God was showing me a future reality, that the pain I was living through was not permanent, and that He had destined me to overcome it. My body in those dreams was like an eagle, and not just any eagle: I was flying *higher* than the eagle itself. It was as if God was whispering, "This is who you really are. This is where you're going. You are not defined by what is happening to you now."

The Bible often uses the eagle as a symbol of strength, freedom, and divine protection. In Isaiah 40:31, we read, *"But those who hope in the Lord will renew their strength. They will soar on wings like eagles; they will run and not grow weary, they will walk and not be faint."* This verse is not only a promise of renewed strength, but also of perspective. Eagles fly high above storms. When other birds flee the winds, eagles rise on them, using the storm itself to lift them higher. My dreams were not random; they were God's way of assuring me that even though storms were raging in my life, they would not destroy me. Instead, those very storms would become the winds that lifted me into my purpose.

What always fascinated me about these dreams was how vivid they were. I could see the world beneath me with clarity, as though my eyes had changed. This, too, is symbolic. The head of an eagle is designed with extraordinary precision. An eagle's eyes are so powerful that they can spot prey from miles away; their vision takes up almost two-thirds of their head's capacity. This design reveals something important about God's message to me: vision is not just about seeing; it's about *knowing*. Knowledge and vision go hand in hand. The eagle is able to act with precision because it first sees with clarity. In the same way, God was showing me that He was giving me not only the ability to rise above but also the clarity to see where I was going — a God-given vision for my life.

This vision was not merely physical sight; it was spiritual insight. As a child enduring trauma, I often felt powerless and unseen. But in my dreams, flying above, I experienced power, freedom, and perspective. Looking down on my life from that height gave me a kind of knowledge I didn't have in the moment: that my suffering had an expiration date, that my pain did not define me, and that God was already shaping my story into something bigger than I could imagine. This is the essence of divine vision — not only seeing what is now, but glimpsing what will be. Like the eagle, I was learning to look beyond the immediate and focus on the eternal.

The more I reflect on the eagle's head, the more I understand how God was teaching me about His nature and my purpose. An eagle's head isn't just large to hold its powerful eyes; it also houses the neurological capacity to process complex information quickly. This allows the eagle to act with precision in real time, whether it's swooping down for prey or navigating turbulent winds. Spiritually, this mirrors what God does when He gives us vision. He doesn't just show us a dream or a glimpse of the future; He also equips us with the wisdom, knowledge, and discernment to navigate life as we move toward that future. In my dreams, God wasn't just showing me a picture of freedom; He was training my heart to understand that freedom, to grow into it, to prepare for it.

There is also humility in this process. Knowing that God has purposed my life does not make me better than anyone else. If anything, it makes me more aware of my dependence on Him. Just as the eagle depends on the wind to soar, I depend on God's Spirit to lift me above my circumstances. In Scripture, God often uses dreams to communicate His plans — think of Joseph, who, as a teenager, dreamed of his future even while he was still in a place of vulnerability and misunderstanding. Like Joseph, I was too young at the time to fully interpret my dreams, but now I see how they fit into God's greater plan for my life. They were not just moments of comfort; they were prophecies of purpose. They were God's way of telling me that He was shaping my destiny even when my reality didn't match the promise.

My story is not about my strength; it's about His faithfulness. Those dreams were not self-made fantasies but God-given revelations. They were God's way of saying, "I have chosen you. I have a plan for you. Even now, I am carrying you above what you're facing." Flying higher than the eagle in my dreams also carries a special significance. The eagle is often seen as the highest standard of strength and freedom, but God was showing me that His plans for me would go beyond even the natural metaphors of strength. Ephesians 3:20 says, *"Now to Him who can do immeasurably more than all we ask or imagine…"* God was illustrating that His purpose for my life would exceed my expectations. It wasn't just about survival; it was about elevation, about becoming a living testament of His power and grace.

This vision -this spiritual knowledge - is what sustains me. Even today, when life presents new challenges, I return to those dreams. They are my reminders that no matter how low my circumstances may feel, God's perspective is always higher. He has given me the eyes of an eagle -eyes to see beyond the moment, eyes to understand that storms are temporary, eyes to know that my purpose is secure. And just as importantly, He has given me the humility to recognize that this vision comes from Him, not from me.

In the end, my story is about God's faithfulness. He spoke to me as a child, not because I was special, but because He is loving. He gave me dreams not because I had earned them, but because He wanted to reassure me of His plan. And He lifted me above my pain, not because I was strong, but because He is mighty. Like the eagle, my life has been shaped to soar — but every lift, every height, every moment of vision has been a gift from Him.

If this book has touched even one heart, it has done its job. My prayer is that you find the strength to rise, the courage to speak your truth, and the faith to walk boldly into your healing. Your story matters. Your voice matters. And no matter how heavy life has felt. You have eagle Wings, Eagle Vision. **My Prayer for You: Rise Like the Eagle**

CHAPTER 8: GRUDGES YOU MUST RELEASE -LEARNING HOW TO HEAL, RELEASE, AND KEEP MOVING

Let It Go and Move Forward: Your Future is Greater Than Your Past

No matter what happens in life, remember this one truth: you live on this earth only once. That alone should remind you how precious your time is, how important your healing is, and how vital it is to make peace with your past so you can move forward into your purpose. It doesn't matter if your childhood was filled with trauma and drama. It doesn't matter if life has introduced you to pain, betrayal, rejection, or loneliness. What matters now is how you choose to respond. You cannot always control what happens to you, but you can absolutely control what you do with it. The decision to let go, forgive, and keep moving forward isn't just a nice idea—it's a requirement if you want to walk in freedom and live the life God destined for you.

One of the greatest lies the enemy tells us is that we must carry our pain forever—that somehow, holding on to our hurt protects us. But truthfully, holding on to pain only weighs us down. Unforgiveness becomes a chain. Bitterness becomes a prison. Anger turns into poison that affects every relationship and decision you make.

Forgiveness is not about excusing what someone did to you. It's about freeing yourself from the burden of carrying it. God didn't design you to walk through life dragging the weight of what was. He designed you to walk in liberty, grace, and purpose. The only way you can truly move forward is to release the past. You cannot walk into your future while gripping the pain of yesterday.

Paul wrote this from a place of deep maturity. He had a past—one filled with mistakes, regret, and even violence. But he understood that his future in Christ was bigger than the pain of his past. You must come to the same conclusion: what God has for you is too important to be delayed by what happened to you. Don't let the memory of pain rob you of present peace. Don't let what someone did to you years ago continue to shape how you see yourself or how you treat others. Your past is not your identity—your purpose is. And God's purpose for your life cannot be fulfilled if you keep looking back.

Forgiveness is not just about letting go of others; it's also about making sure your own heart stays clean. Psalm 51:10 *"Create in me a clean heart, O God, and renew a right spirit within me."*

When people mistreat you, it's tempting to let bitterness or revenge settle in. But if you want to walk with God, you must ask Him to keep your heart soft, clean, and right—even toward those who wronged you. This doesn't mean you deny the pain. It means you choose to let God heal it instead of letting it turn you into someone you were never meant to be.

Your heart determines the course of your life. A hardened, bitter heart will always block you from experiencing the fullness of God's blessings. But a pure heart? That kind of heart invites the presence of God and opens doors to divine favor.

Treat People Right—Even If They Don't Deserve It

Jesus said in Luke 6:27-28: *"But to you who are listening I say: Love your enemies, do good to those who hate you, bless those who curse you, pray for those who mistreat you."*

That's not easy. Especially when people have deeply hurt you, but remember, your obedience to God is not based on how others behave. It's based on your relationship with Him. How you treat people—especially those who mistreat you—reflects your maturity and trust in God to defend and vindicate you. Forgiveness doesn't mean access. You can forgive someone and still maintain healthy boundaries. You can love someone and still move forward without them in your life. But you must always choose righteousness over resentment. You must decide that bitterness won't live in your spirit.

Yes, it hurts. Yes, you might have to walk through a lonely season. Yes, you might have to cry, grieve, and wrestle with what happened. But healing is possible—and it's promised.

Psalm 34:18 reminds us: *"The Lord is close to the brokenhearted and saves those who are crushed in spirit."*

You may feel alone, but you are not abandoned. God is with you in the quiet moments, in the sleepless nights, in the painful memories. He's not just watching from a distance—He is near, restoring, mending, and strengthening you for what's next. Sometimes the lonely space is necessary. It's in that space where you get clarity. It's in that space where you shed old mindsets. It's in that space where God prepares you for elevation.

There comes a point where you have to stop replaying the pain. Stop rehearsing what happened. Stop asking why they did it, why it turned out that way, or what could have been different. You will never discover your future if your mind is stuck in the past. Think of Lot's wife. In Genesis 19, God was delivering Lot and his family from destruction, but she looked back—and was turned into a pillar of salt. Why? Because she couldn't let go of what was. She had a future, but her attachment to the past destroyed her destiny. Don't make the same mistake. Move forward—and don't look back.

Isaiah 43:18-19 says: *"Forget the former things; do not dwell on the past. See, I am doing a new thing! Now it springs up; do you not perceive it?"*

God is doing something new in your life. A new chapter. A new opportunity. A new level of healing, growth, and purpose. Destiny is more than a dream, a desire, or even a goal. It is the divine purpose for which you were created. Destiny is God's original intention for your life—what He wrote about you before you ever took your first breath. It is the unique path, calling, and assignment designed just for you. Destiny is not random; it is deliberate. God, in His infinite wisdom, wove your life into the fabric of history for a reason. You are here on purpose, for purpose. God knows you, sees you, and has already established what you are meant to become. But although destiny is divinely given, it must be walked out. And here's the truth: while nothing and no one can cancel what God has planned for your life, you can delay it, resist it, or block it.

What Blocks Destiny?

When *"destiny is calling,"* I am speaking of a spiritual awakening, a divine moment when your life begins to align with the purpose for which you were created. It's that inner pull, that unshakable feeling, that there is **more** to your existence than what you've experienced so far. It's a season where God begins to stir your spirit, open your eyes, and prompt you to move forward, to rise above past limitations, and to become who He always intended you to be. Destiny calling is not just about success, money, or recognition. It's about **fulfilling God's purpose** for your life. It's the moment your gifts, your pain, your lessons, and your faith come together to push you into a new level of meaning and impact.

Every person is born with a destiny—God doesn't create without purpose. Your destiny is the divine assignment placed on your life before you were born. Psalm 139:16 says: *"All the days ordained for me were written in your book before one of them came to be."* That means God already had a plan when He formed you. When destiny calls, it is a signal that it's time to start walking in that plan, not just existing, but living intentionally, with purpose and direction.

When destiny is calling, you often feel a "holy discontent." You begin to feel uncomfortable with where you are. What once satisfied you no longer fulfills you. You sense that there's more—more you're capable of, more God wants to do through you. It's as if God is tapping you on the shoulder and saying, *"Get ready. I'm taking you somewhere new."* This discomfort isn't to frustrate you—it's to **stretch you**, to prepare you for the next level. It's God pulling you out of comfort zones so He can launch you into greater things.

When destiny calls, you must decide: **Will you answer?**

Many people feel the call of destiny but never walk in it because it requires obedience, sacrifice, healing, and letting go. It means you may have to release toxic relationships, old habits, grudges, and even fear. It means trusting God with the unknown and stepping into what feels unfamiliar. Abraham answered destiny's call when God told him to leave his homeland. Esther answered when she risked her life to save her people. Jesus fulfilled His destiny when He surrendered to the cross. In every case, **obedience is the unlocked purpose**. Your destiny will never pull you backward. It always calls you **higher**—to grow, to stretch, to heal, to love, and to serve. It calls you to be a light in dark places, to be a blessing in someone else's life, and to walk in the fullness of your identity in Christ.

There are many things that can hinder you from stepping fully into your God-ordained destiny:

- Fear of failure or rejection
- Unforgiveness and emotional wounds
- Disobedience to God's instructions
- Negative mindsets or limiting beliefs
- Toxic relationships
- Unrepented sin
- And perhaps one of the most dangerous: **grudges and bitterness**

You cannot step into a divine future while dragging the baggage of your past. Grudges—whether against others, yourself, or even against God can become a **spiritual roadblock**. They take up space in your heart where peace, wisdom, and discernment should live. They cloud your judgment, drain your energy, and make you stuck in cycles of emotional pain. When destiny is calling, it's time to move. Don't ignore it. Don't delay. It is time now.

Grudges: A Silent Destiny Killer. Grudges may seem harmless at first—a silent resentment, a memory you revisit now and then, a justified anger. But over time, grudges grow roots. They harden your heart. They poison your thoughts. They keep you rehearsing old wounds instead of embracing new opportunities. And eventually, they make you unavailable for the new things God wants to do in your life. Bitterness doesn't just trouble you—it affects your relationships, your faith, your vision, and your ability to hear from God clearly.

You cannot carry both a grudge and your destiny. One will have to go. God calls you to **release others**, not because they always deserve it, but because **you do**. You deserve to be free. You deserve to heal. You deserve to step into the full life God has prepared for you. Forgiveness is the key that unlocks the door to your next season. Releasing grudges doesn't mean what happened was okay—it means you've decided to stop letting it control you.

When you let go, you make space for **joy**, **peace**, and **purpose** to flow again. You give God room to restore and elevate you. And you posture yourself to walk fully in the destiny He designed for you. Destiny is calling. But you must travel light. Lay down the weight of old pain. Release the bitterness. Forgive me freely. And walk forward with a clean heart and open hands. Your future is too important to let the past hold you hostage.

God has not changed His mind about your destiny—but it's time you stop letting grudges keep you from it. You are a vessel of purpose. You were designed for impact, for legacy, for light. Every painful experience you endured is not wasted—it becomes fuel for your calling. That includes the trauma, the betrayal, the nights you thought you wouldn't make it. God is working it all together—not to break you, but to build you. Your destiny is ahead of you, not behind you. Your future is bright. And your best days are still to come. Don't hold grudges. Don't allow anger or resentment to take root. Choose peace. Choose forgiveness. Choose growth. Choose to move—and keep moving.

I am not what happened to me; I am what God is calling me to be. I release the past, I forgive, and I press forward. My heart is clean, my spirit is right, and my steps are ordered. I choose freedom. I choose healing. I choose purpose. In Jesus' name, Amen.

CHAPTER 9: CHILD, PLEASE – YOU CAN MAKE IT

"Child, please" - My Cry and My Praise

You ask me why I trust God the way I do — why I serve Him with my whole heart, why I bless others even when I'm in pain, why I dance and praise with tears in my eyes and fire in my spirit. *Child, please.* If you only knew. That phrase isn't just a saying — it's a cry that stretches from my childhood to this very moment. It holds the weight of my story. Because every single day of my life, God has *kept* me. In the middle of dysfunction, rejection, and silent battles, He never let go.

I wasn't spared from pain. I came from a home where dysfunction echoed in the walls. But Love was not absent. I stepped into workplaces where wickedness was hidden behind titles. I've been laughed at because of my childhood issues with obesity and ignored. Due to other insecurities and fear of the favor that was evident in my life, Counted Out, But Called By God: Becoming Better, Not Bitter. There was a time when I was counted out—pushed aside, overlooked, underestimated. Not because I lacked potential, but because others couldn't see what God had already placed inside me. They saw a child, small in voice but great in calling. They saw weakness where God had planted strength. They tried to silence me—not just my voice, but my purpose—because they knew that if truth ever came out, **it would speak louder than their lies.**

Fear often tries to silence what it cannot control. And integrity? It terrifies those who live behind deception. So I was silenced—not by choice, but by pressure. Made to feel like my truth didn't matter. Made to believe that if I spoke up, I would be shamed, blamed, or broken. But here's what they didn't know: **God was still writing.**

The silence didn't destroy me; it developed me. The rejection didn't ruin me; it refined me. Every plot, every scheme, every attempt to keep me down only positioned me for elevation. And now I understand—**what was meant to break me actually built me.**

Yes, I was counted out—but not by God. Yes, they tried to silence me—but God gave me a new sound. Yes, they hoped I'd grow bitter—but **God made me better.**

Bitterness is a choice, and I chose not to drink that poison. I chose healing over hatred. I chose freedom over offense. And it wasn't always easy. Bitterness knocks at the door of every wounded heart. But I decided that I wouldn't let what they did become who I am. Because when God is with you, **you don't**

have to prove yourself—He will prove you. And when He heals you, you no longer carry the weight of trying to get even. You rise above, not in pride, but in peace.

That's why I can **bless those who plotted against me.** That's why I can **pray for those who schemed and slandered.**
That's why I can **walk in love when I have every reason to hate.**

Not because I'm strong in myself—but because **God has made me whole.**

Matthew 5:44 says: *"But I say to you, love your enemies and pray for those who persecute you."*

That's not weakness—that's power. That's a heart so secure in God that it doesn't need revenge. That's someone who knows **God is the lifter of their head**, the defender of their name, and the restorer of all things. I stand today not because people lifted me, but because **God raised me.** I didn't climb here on approval—I rose on grace. And I don't carry bitterness—I carry blessings. Because of God, I am above—not in arrogance, but in assignment. He has elevated me out of the pit and into purpose. He has anointed me to do what others thought I never could. And He's using my story—not the perfect version, but the real, raw, redeemed story—to bring freedom to others.

Psalm 23:5 says: *"You prepare a table before me in the presence of my enemies. You anoint my head with oil; my cup overflows."*

That's not just verse, that's my testimony.

But never forgotten by God. Through it all, He gave me a gift of **discernment**. A knowing in my spirit that helped me see beyond smiles and into the truth. It protected me from traps meant to destroy me. It kept me from attaching to the wrong people and guided me toward the right ones. And even when the enemy tried to break me, God surrounded me with *God-given fathers, mothers, and families* — people who showed me a different way to live, love, and hope. They were evidence that God was rewriting my story.

Please let me be clear: my confidence is not arrogance. It's not pride in self — it's certainty in *God*. It's the quiet boldness that comes from knowing I should've been taken out a long time ago… but God kept me. I've been through too much, survived too much, lost too much — and yet here I stand. This confidence is not performance; it's proof. Proof that God covered me when I couldn't cover myself. Proof that grace carried me when strength ran out. It's not that I think I'm better than anyone — it's that I *know* God was better to me than I deserved. That assurance? It humbles me every time.

So yes — I'm moving with urgency. I don't have time to waste or space **to play small**. This urgency is not stress; it's *honor*. It's my offering to God. I work while it is day, not because I'm hustling for approval, but because I understand the value of the time I've been given. Every door He opens, I walk through. Every assignment He gives, I complete with diligence. I know what it feels like to live in delay, to survive seasons where everything felt stuck — so when He says *"Go,"* I don't hesitate. My urgency is my *thank you*. My obedience is my worship. The pressure I feel is not from people — it's from purpose. And I'm determined to give God a full return on the breath He's put in my lungs.

And no solitude is not arrogance either. A decision to protect your peace, to limit crowds, to preserve your inner circle — that's not pride, that's *wisdom*. I guard my heart because my heart is where God speaks. I guard my spirit because I carry something holy. I've learned that not everyone can go where God is taking me, and that's okay. I don't isolate to elevate myself — I separate to *consecrate*. I need quiet to hear clearly. I need discernment to move wisely. I'd rather be misunderstood by man than disconnected from God. Because when I stand before Him, I want to know I served Him well — not distracted, not drained, but devoted.

So when you see me praise, understand this: I'm not dancing because life has been easy. I'm dancing because grace met me in the fire and carried me out. I'm praising because God *revealed* that I would rise — not by my strength, but by leaning and depending fully on Him. I'm still here because He rescued me — not once, but over and over again. So *child, please* — don't count yourself out. If He did it for me, He can do it for you. You *can* make it. You *will* rise.

Because, as the Word says, **"Many are the afflictions of the righteous, but the Lord delivers him out of them all."** — *Psalm 34:19*

Let me tell you something right now: **You are not your past.** You are not your pain. You are not the lies spoken over you, the trauma that tried to define you, or the fear that tried to hold you hostage. And no matter what anyone told you, you *can* make it. I don't say that lightly. I say it because I've lived it. I know what it's like to be hurt, overlooked, underestimated, misunderstood, and deeply broken.

They say your childhood shapes you, but no one talks about what happens when it nearly breaks you. When the dysfunction you were born into feels like a curse you didn't ask for. When you grow up learning survival instead of safety. When love feels inconsistent, and validation is something you have to chase. That kind of pain leaves invisible bruises. You walk through life trying to smile while silently wondering if you'll ever feel whole. *But God.*

God stepped into the places no one else could reach. He saw what I couldn't even say. He heard the prayers I didn't have words for. He met me not at my best, but at my breaking point — and instead of rejecting me, He rebuilt me. Piece by piece. Layer by layer. Grace by grace. And through it all, I've come to know this truth: **With God, nothing is wasted.** Every wound, every tear, every silent night — He uses it to grow something greater. My pain became my platform. My struggle became my strength. My story became an invitation to hope.

Moving forward with confidence in who God has created you to be is not only a blessing to yourself but a powerful way to impact the lives of others. In Philippians 3:13-14, Paul encourages us to "forget what is behind and strain toward what is ahead." This means that regardless of past struggles, doubts, or challenges, we are called to press forward with purpose and to celebrate the unique person God has shaped us to be. Embrace your journey, understanding that each step forward is a step in fulfilling God's plan for you, a plan that will bless others through your actions, words, and presence.

Celebrating yourself is not an act of arrogance but a recognition of God's faithfulness in your life. When you celebrate who you are, you honor the Creator who designed you with love, intention, and grace. Psalm 118:24 reminds us that "This is the day the Lord has made; let us rejoice and be glad in it." Rejoicing in yourself is an acknowledgment that you are fearfully and wonderfully made. As you stand tall in your identity, free from the constraints of comparison or insecurity, you radiate that joy and peace to those around you. The more you celebrate your unique gifts and qualities, the more you encourage others to do the same, creating an environment of mutual support, growth, and encouragement.

As you move forward in this journey, you become a living testament to God's goodness, and your life becomes a blessing to others. Jesus calls us to love our neighbors as ourselves (Mark 12:31), and part of loving others well is first learning to love and appreciate ourselves in the way God intended. When you move forward with purpose, embracing the fullness of who you are, you make space for others to step into their own greatness. Your journey of growth, empowerment, and celebration becomes a catalyst for the growth of those around you. So move forward confidently, celebrate your progress, and know that in doing so, you are shining a light that encourages and uplifts the world around you.

You are *loved*—a truth so deep and transformative that it can change the very core of who you are. In moments of despair, when everything else seems to fail, love remains the constant, unshakable force that lifts us from the depths of our struggles. 1 Corinthians 13:7 tells us that love "bears all things, believes all things, hopes all things, endures all things." Love, as shown through God's grace, is the lifter that holds us up when we are weak. It doesn't falter, doesn't fail, and it always has the power to lift us higher, reminding us that no matter the circumstances, we are never alone. God's love is a sure foundation that can carry us through any storm.

However, to fully experience the transformative power of love, we must first understand what love truly looks and feels like. Too often, the world distorts love, equating it with fleeting emotions or conditional affection. But God's love is unconditional, unchanging, and perfect. In 1 John 4:9-10, it is written: "This is how God showed his love among us: He sent his one and only Son into the world that we might live through him. This is love: not that we loved God, but that he loved us and sent his Son as an atoning sacrifice for our sins." God's love is sacrificial, selfless, and it doesn't require us to be perfect. When we receive this love in its purest form, we begin to understand that it's not about what we do, but about who God is and how He sees us.

Receiving God's love is the foundation that enables us to pass His love on to others. When we grasp the depth of God's love for us, we are empowered to reflect that love outwardly. Jesus taught us to love one another as He has loved us (John 13:34), and by accepting His love, we can give that same love to others. Love is not just an emotion; it's an action. It's being present, offering grace, speaking kindness, and showing compassion. By allowing God's love to fill our hearts, we become vessels of His love, passing it along to others in tangible ways. And as we share His love, it becomes a cycle of healing, encouragement, and growth, reminding us all that we are never beyond the reach of God's perfect love.

I often leaned on my mother's prayers—her words, her faith, and her unwavering belief that God would carry me, even when I couldn't carry myself. She was a true prayer warrior, the kind of woman who could shift atmospheres with a whisper to heaven. In times when I felt lost, broken, or unsure, her prayers wrapped around me like a shield. Her encouragement and wisdom were like light in my darkest moments, and no matter what I was going through, she'd always end with the same powerful words: *"Child, please… God got you."* Back then, I heard it as comfort—but now, I *know* it was prophetic truth.

What I once thought was the sound of my cry—raw, weary, and desperate—was really the sound of my *praise* rising from the depths of my spirit. I used to believe that my tears were a sign of weakness, but now I realize they were a form of worship, a release of faith when I had no words left. Romans 8:26 reminds us that the Spirit intercedes for us with groanings too deep for words. My cry was never just sorrow; it was surrender. And in that surrender, I was praising through the pain, worshipping through the confusion, and unknowingly echoing the same faith my mother had always shown me.

Now I stand stronger, with a deeper understanding of her words—*"God got you."* It wasn't just a saying; it was a declaration of divine assurance. It means that no matter what life throws your way, you're held, you're seen, and you're sustained by a God who never fails. My mother's prayers didn't just protect me—they planted seeds of faith that are now bearing fruit in my own life.

When a baby cries, it's never without meaning. That cry is their only way of communicating a need, whether it's hunger, comfort, protection, or simply the reassurance of a loving presence. The cry is instinctive, raw, and honest. And just like a mother or father responds to that cry, God listens to ours with even greater attentiveness and care. Psalm 34:17 says, *"The righteous cry out, and the Lord hears them; He delivers them from all their troubles."* Just as a parent moves swiftly at the sound of their child's cry, God responds to us with compassion, provision, and love. He never ignores our cries—He interprets them, even when we don't fully understand what we need ourselves.

As we grow, we often learn to suppress our cries, thinking they make us look weak. But in the eyes of God, our cry is not weakness—it's a relationship. It's trust. It's a sign that we know where to run when we're in need. Just as a child trusts that their parent will respond, our spiritual cry acknowledges that we know our Father hears us. Romans 8:15 reminds us, *"The Spirit you received brought about your adoption to sonship. And by him we cry, 'Abba, Father.'"* Our cries, whether silent or loud, are powerful expressions of connection to the One who holds all answers. They're not just calls for help-they're declarations of dependency and faith.

When my mother would say, *"Child, please… God got you,"* it wasn't just a comforting phrase—it was a holy reminder that, just like an attentive parent to a crying infant, God is always ready to respond. The cry is not the end; it is the beginning of

God's movement in your life. He sees what you need, even before you speak it. Isaiah 65:24 says, *"Before they call, I will answer; while they are still speaking, I will hear."* Your cry reaches the throne of heaven, and God—your Father—is already on the way. Whether it's peace, strength, healing, or direction, He hears you. And not only does He hear, you can rest assured that He *got you*.

So I say to myself, and to anyone who's ever leaned on the prayers of someone before them: *Child, please... God got you.* And even when all you can do is cry, know that Heaven hears you—and that might just be your greatest praise.

When I tell you that you can make it, I'm not just giving you pretty words. I'm giving you *proof.* I am living, breathing evidence that God still heals. Still restore. Still makes everything new. Yes, your past may have shaped you, but it doesn't define you. It doesn't cancel your future. It doesn't disqualify your call. You are not too far gone. You are not too damaged. You are still chosen. Still called. Still covered. Everything I went through — the silent tears, the battles nobody knew about, the storms I thought would drown me — God used it all to build me, strengthen me, and prepare me. What the enemy meant for harm, God turned into training. He took my scars and made them a testimony. He took my weakness and filled it with His power. And if He did it for me, He can do it for you. You are not disqualified. You're not too late.

Unshakable Joy and Unbothered Grace

When you see me smiling in moments when you think a frown would be more appropriate, understand this — it's not denial, it's divine joy. The joy that God gives cannot be removed, replaced, or destroyed by circumstances. My smile isn't fake; it's faith. It's a reflection of peace that didn't come from people, so people cannot take it away.

"The joy of the Lord is your strength. "That's not just a verse to me — it's my reality. God's joy has become my anchor. It holds me steady when life tries to shake me. It reminds me that no matter what I face, I am never without strength, never without reason to smile.

I am not moved because you may dislike me — perhaps because of your own insecurities — understand, it's not that I don't care; it's that I've already overcome *dislike*. I've learned that people's opinions do not define my identity. Your rejection does not diminish my worth. Your silence cannot cancel my purpose. I rest in that truth. I no longer carry the heavy weight of needing to be liked by everyone. I have peace in knowing that God's approval is enough.

If you don't understand why *lies* don't shake me, know this — it's not arrogance, it's assurance. A lie is not my problem; it's the liar's issue. I refuse to wrestle with what God has already handled. The truth always has a way of standing tall when everything else falls apart. **John 8:32** says, "And ye shall know the truth, and the truth shall make you free." That freedom means I don't have to defend myself; I just have to stay in alignment with God.

I realize that ignoring me is you, not me. I don't take offense. I don't shrink, and I don't retaliate. I've learned that being ignored doesn't mean I'm not there — it simply reveals more about your discomfort than my presence. I don't need to know what to have worth. God saw me when nobody else did. Life has already taught me how to handle you with love and to keep moving with purpose. Every trial, every betrayal, every silent room has trained me not to react, but to *respond* with grace. I've discovered that love is not a feeling — it's a decision. It's choosing to be kind when others are cruel, choosing to forgive when others accuse, and choosing peace when others bring confusion. Though You slay me, yet will I trust Him" (**Job 13:15**) is a declaration of unshakable faith — the kind that remains steadfast even when life feels unbearable. Job's words remind us that trust in God is not based on comfort or understanding, but on confidence in His character. **Matthew 5:44** commands us, "But I say unto you, Love your enemies, bless them that curse you, do good to them that hate you, and pray for them which despitefully use you, and persecute you." That verse is not easy to live, but it's powerful when you do because love disarms what hate tries to fuel.

So, if you see me smiling, unmoved, unbothered, understand this — it's not pride, it's peace. It's not arrogance, it's awareness. I've learned who I am in God, and I refuse to let anyone pull me back. Discernment allows you to have assurance that.

I walk with joy because I've already cried enough tears. I move with grace because I've already wrestled with pain. I love it right because I've seen what happens when you don't. Discernment is one of God's greatest gifts — it allows us to *see* beyond what is said, to *understand* beyond what is shown, and to *love* beyond what is deserved. True discernment doesn't make us judgmental; it makes us wise. It opens our spiritual eyes to the deeper truth of people and situations, revealing their pain, motives, or struggles without hardening our hearts toward them. **Hebrews 5:14** says, *"But solid food belongs to those* *who are of full age, that is, those who by reason of use have their senses exercised to discern both good and evil."* When we walk in discernment, we don't react out of offense or emotion — we respond out of wisdom and compassion. We recognize that some actions come from hurt, not hatred, from confusion, not character.

Discernment allows us to love rightly. It teaches us how to set healthy boundaries while still walking in grace. It helps us forgive quickly because we understand that people often act from what they have been through, not from who they truly are. When we see through God's eyes, we stop taking everything personally and start praying more intentionally. We don't have to agree with or accept every behavior, but we can still reflect God's heart in how we handle it. That's the beauty of discernment — it keeps us wise enough to recognize truth and loving enough to still extend grace.

Life taught me to let God fight my battles, and now I just live in victory — smiling, loving, and walking in purpose. Even when everything is falling apart, true faith says, *"I may not see what You're doing, God, but I still believe You're good."* Trusting God in pain transforms suffering into purpose because we know He can bring beauty out of ashes. This kind of faith doesn't deny the hurt — it endures through it, knowing that God's plan is greater than the present pain.

As you walk in the purpose of God for your life, fear no evil — for truly, *God is with you.* When His hand is upon you, no weapon formed against you can prosper (**Isaiah 54:17**). The presence of God becomes your shield, your comfort, and your confidence. You no longer walk in fear because you understand that your steps are ordered by the Lord (**Psalm 37:23**). Every experience, even the painful ones, is being used to shape you for destiny. What once tried to break you now becomes the very thing that builds you.

Your past has nothing to do with your future when you are walking with God. He specializes in rewriting stories and redeeming what was once lost. The world may try to remind you of who you were, but God keeps speaking to who you are becoming. **2 Corinthians 5:17** declares, *"Therefore if any man be in Christ, he is a new creature: old things are passed away; behold, all things are become new."* God's plan is the plan — not man's opinion, not your mistakes, not your fears. When you surrender fully to His purpose, He transforms every detour into destiny and every setback into a setup for greater things.

Even when darkness surrounded you, that dream of flying high was God whispering, *"You will rise."* It was His assurance that the pit would not be your prison and the storm would not be your end. What was meant to smother you became the wind that lifted you higher. You were never meant to crawl where God designed you to soar. As **Isaiah 40:31** reminds us, *"But they that wait upon the Lord shall renew their strength; they shall mount up with wings as eagles."* You were made to fly above fear, above doubt, above everything not designed by God — moving boldly in purpose, carried by His strength, and sustained by His love.

You're not too broken. God can still write beauty from your ashes.

This chapter isn't just my story; it's an invitation for you. A reminder that you can rise. You *will* heal. And what the enemy meant for evil, God will use for your good.

Child, please with God, you can make it.

YOU CAN MAKE IT!

ANCHOR SCRIPTURES FOR DR SHARLI K. ADAIR

1. **Psalm 34:17-18** – *"The righteous cry out, and the Lord hears them; he delivers them from all their troubles. The Lord is close to the brokenhearted and saves those who are crushed in spirit."*
2. **Romans 8:28** – *"And we know that in all things God works for the good of those who love him, who have been called according to his purpose."*
3. **Isaiah 41:10** – *"So do not fear, for I am with you; do not be dismayed, for I am your God. I will strengthen you and help you; I will uphold you with my righteous right hand."*
4. **2 Corinthians 12:9-10** – *"But he said to me, 'My grace is sufficient for you, for my power is made perfect in weakness.' Therefore, I will boast all the more gladly about my weaknesses, so that Christ's power may rest on me."*
5. **Jeremiah 29:11** – *"For I know the plans I have for you,' declares the Lord, 'plans to prosper you and not to harm you, plans to give you hope and a future."*

This book is a testimony that God speaks to children in dreams, and that dreams come true no matter what life looks like.

CLOSING PRAYER

Lord God,

Thank You for being the God who speaks, who saves, and who lifts us high when life tries to hold us down. Just like You gave me dreams of soaring, I know you have planted vision and purpose in the hearts of others — even in the middle of fear, trauma, or confusion. I pray for every person who reads or hears this testimony: that they would know they are seen, chosen, and loved by You. Teach them to trust Your timing, to believe in the vision You've given them, and to rise with the strength of an eagle — or even higher. Keep their eyes clear, their hearts humble, and their purpose firm in You.

In the mighty name of Jesus,

Dr. Sharli Kay Marlow- Adair

ACKNOWLEDGEMENT

Thank you to: my beautiful daughter Ivi D'vynne, Dr. Marcia Smith, My awesome son in love – Mr. Jaspierre Smith. My awesome Grandsons Jaspierre Jr. and Jayceaon

www.ingramcontent.com/pod-product-compliance
Lightning Source LLC
Chambersburg PA
CBHW042329150426
43193CB00005B/56